The A to Z of (A)

by

Robert Cubitt

© 2020

Having purchased this eBook from Amazon, it is for your personal use only. It may not be copied, reproduced, printed or used in any way, other than in its intended Kindle format.

Published by Selfishgenie Publishing of, Northamptonshire, England.

Nothing is intended or should be interpreted as representing or expressing the views and policies of any department or agency of any government or other body.

All trademarks used are the property of their respective owners. All trademarks are recognised.

The right of Robert Cubitt to be identified as the author of this work has been asserted in accordance with sections 77 and 78 of the Copyright Designs and Patents Act 1988.

Other titles by the Same Author

Fiction
The Deputy Prime Minister
The Inconvenience Store
The Charity Thieves

Warriors Series
The Warriors: The Girl I Left Behind Me
The Warriors: Mirror Man

The Magi Series
The Magi
Genghis Kant (The Magi Book 2)
New Earth (The Magi Book 3)
Cloning Around (The Magi Book 4)
Timeslip (The Magi Book 5)
The Return Of Su Mali (The Magi Book 6)
Robinson Kohli (The Magi Book 7)
Parallel Lines (The Magi Book 8)

Carter's Commandos Series
Operation Absalom (Carter's Commandos Book 1)
Operation Tightrope (Carter's Commandos Book 2)

Non-Fiction
A Commando's Story
I'm So Glad You Asked Me That
I Want That Job

Contents

Illustrations
Foreword
Introduction
The A to Z Terminology
Final Words
Acknowledgements
Sources
And Now

Illustrations

My thanks go to Ivan Zamyslov, who plies his artistic trade under the name of Azante, for providing the illustrations used in this book. Ivan has also illustrated a number of children's books. Anyone needing the services of an illustrator can contact Ivan through the Fiverr website using this link. https://www.fiverr.com/azante

Foreword

By Tiger Woods

When I was invited to write the foreword for this book by my old friend, Bob Cubitt, I was extremely flattered. Not only is Bob Cubitt a world expert in amateur golf, he's a really great guy.

In reading this book the first thing I noticed was the great attention to detail that has been taken. Not only does Bob understand amateur golf, he understands the minutiae of the game. The next thing I noticed was the subtlety of his observations. Not only does he understand the game, but he understands the people who play and manage the game.

Finally, I understood Bob's passion for the game. Golf is in his blood and his very soul. In fact I would go so far as to say that Bob Cubitt is amateur golf personified.

So, I am delighted to recommend this book to all current amateur golfers and to all those who would wish to emulate Bob and become an amateur golfer.

Author's note: I am legally obliged to point out that the Tiger Woods who wrote the above foreword is not Eldrick Tont "Tiger" Woods, the world famous golfer, but is Timothy "Tiger" Woods, who drinks with me in the Dog and Duck in Little Swampflats.

Introduction

I love the game of golf and I love writing, so it was inevitable that the two parts of this Venn diagram should one day overlap into a book about golf. It is, I hope, part humorous, part historical, part golfing dictionary and part autobiographical, given that it contains a lot of my own golfing stories. This book is aimed very much at the amateur golfer and would-be amateur golfers, not at those who are professional golfers, or those who aspire to become professionals. I would go so far as to say it isn't even aimed at those who would aspire to play on a sub 10 handicap (see *Handicap*).

There is a difference between the true amateur and those who are at the top of the game. They may use similar equipment, they may even wear similar clothes, but those who are good enough to play on a low handicap or even make money from the game, are a different breed. They are the Albert Einstein's of the game, compared to the GCSE science students. The gulf between the amateur and those at the top of the game, such as Tiger Woods, Rory McIlroy and the guy whose name I can't even pronounce, let alone spell (**Editor's note**: He means Xander Schauffele), is so big that you can't see to the other side. They look down on the average club golfers like the Gods on Olympus looking down on mortal men.

If you are one of those at the top of the game, please feel free to buy this book, of course, but don't expect to learn that much from it.

No, this book is aimed at those players who haunt the golf courses of the world, seeking that perfect game that will one day result in them winning the monthly medal (3rd Division) (see *Monthly Medal*) or have their name inscribed on the "Honours Board" in the club house for being the fourth member of the Four Ball (see *Four ball*) that won the Captain's Charity Trophy, when only three scores counted anyway.

How to tell if you are a true amateur golfer (tick just one to qualify):

- You will tell your playing partners to ignore the lightning because you are about to putt out for a par.

- You will seek relief from "temporary water" (see *Water*) when the country is going through the longest dry spell in its history.

- You will humble-brag to your playing partners that you think your handicap should be lower, when in fact you would give your eye teeth for it to go up by two strokes.

- You think that not being last in a competition is as good as winning it.

- While waiting for the green keeper to finish mowing the teeing area (see *Teeing area*), you suggest he replaces the markers forward by two feet.

- You constantly complain about slow play, while taking your tenth practice swing.

- You seriously considered booking a tee-time for Christmas Day.

- It takes you longer to describe the great putt you made than it did to actually make the putt.

- You know that when practicing your putting on the living room carpet, the ball will break away from walls but towards furniture.

- You think the coffee in the clubhouse is overpriced.

As with the game of golf itself, there are some rules that must be applied when reading this book.

1. Take everything you read in this book with a huge measure of salt. References to the sources I consulted are included at the end and can provide more definitive answers than you may find here.

2. If in doubt, consult the Rules of Golf (RoG from here on. See *Rules of Golf*), as issued by the R&A (see *R&A*). Where specific rule numbers are quoted, they are the rules in force in January 2020 and may have changed (again) by the time you read this book.

3. Don't quote this book to the committee of your golf club. Especially don't mention my name to them.

4. Don't take this book too seriously.

That last rule is probably the most important of all. However, there is some serious stuff in here. Just skip over that when you get to it.

What can you expect from this book?

Golf, like many other sports and pastimes, has its own language, or jargon. Understanding that language can be an impediment for people taking up the game. In researching this book, I have come across terms I hadn't heard before and I've been playing the game for over forty years. So, this book seeks to filter some of the mud out of the water and provide some clarity. It also tells some stories, some of which may or may not be funny. If you chuckle, they were meant to be funny. If you fail to chuckle, they weren't meant to be funny.

There are other A to Z lists available that tell you what golfing terms mean, but this one goes deeper. It doesn't just tell you what the words mean, it tells you what they mean in practical terms. For example, under the listing for Pro Shop it will tell you why you go in there intending only to book a tee time and walk out with a brand new set of golf clubs that you didn't even know you needed.

You will also get some of the history of the terms. Yes, we know that "fore" is what you shout to warn other golfers that your ball is heading straight at them. But why do we use that word and not some other word?

You will also get a few anecdotes from my own golfing experience and a few told to me by other golfers and you can be certain that you'll get more than a few of my own opinions. Put it all together and you get what might be described as a "bluffer's guide" to the game of golf, suitable for use even by non-golfers. But I think that phrase has been made copyright, so I've had to call this an A to Z instead, on the grounds that you can't copyright letters of the alphabet.

So, what is golf? Well, the RoG describes it as follows:

"Golf is played in a round of 18 (or fewer) holes on a course by striking a ball with a club.
Each hole starts with a stroke from the teeing area and ends when the ball is holed on the putting green (or when the Rules otherwise say the hole is completed)."

So far, so bland, because for an amateur golfer the game is so much more than just getting a ball from tee (see *Tee*) to green (see *Green*) eighteen times.

For most amateurs, golf is their hobby and pastime. For many amateurs, the game is a way for them to get fresh air and exercise. For many more it is the centre of their social life. For some it is a way to escape their spouse, while for others it is a way of doing something together with their spouse. For a sad few, it is a way to fill a few hours of an otherwise empty day.

That is what makes the amateur different from the professional. For the professional, golf is a way to use their talents to make money. And, make no mistake, that is a big difference. Most professionals would play the game anyway, I am sure, but to play the game in the middle of winter with no hope of making money requires motivation of another sort. And millions of us play the game in the middle of winter for no reason other than our love of the game.

If you learn anything from this book I will be delighted; in fact I'll be amazed. But please remember, this book is written with a heart full of love for the game of golf as it is played by we amateurs - the people who actually keep the game alive when the TV cameras have all been packed away and the spectators have all gone home.

Bob Cubitt
Northamptonshire
2020.

Authors Note: Some terminology used in this book is different in the USA and where I have referred to money, I haven't always converted from dollars to pounds and vice versa. I haven't converted to Euros at all (We're British, dammit!). Please accept my apologies, but I was writing this in a rush to get back on the golf course and didn't have the time to make all the necessary changes.

A typical amateur golfer

A is For

Abnormal course conditions

Abnormal course conditions are any conditions that the amateur golfer doesn't like. He will seek to take relief (see *Relief*) from those conditions despite his playing partners telling him he can't.

The true golfer will then consult the rule book, which he or she always carries with them (**Editor's note**: that's a lie, for a start). The most common type of abnormal course conditions encountered by golfers is holes created by animals, so they will claim that a divot (see *Divot*) caused by another golfer is actually a hole created by an animal.

If the golfer is less dedicated and therefore not carrying a copy of the rule book, they will tell a story about a mate of theirs who was given relief in similar circumstances. Only the golfer himself will know if the story is true. But it doesn't matter because an anecdote can never supersede the rules of golf.

As the rules regarding abnormal course conditions are quite well defined, the golfer's partners can expect quite a long debate on this subject before they eventually concede in order to shut the golfer up and get back to the clubhouse (see *Clubhouse*) before the bar closes or it gets dark, whichever is the sooner.

Accessories

There is a difference between "accessories" and "aids" (see *Aids*). The use of aids is covered by the rules of golf, whereas the use of accessories is not.

If you want to become a millionaire, invent an accessory that the amateur will want to buy. If you can promise that it will increase the distance they can hit the ball, the accuracy of their putting, or improve their swing, you will become rich beyond the dreams of avarice. The key to this claim is that the amateur is unable to prove that this hasn't happened because the skill of the individual is actually the deciding factor, therefore you don't have to refund their money when improvements fail to emerge.

Of course, some golfing accessories are necessary. Most golfers need gloves, towels, tee pegs and a hundred other small items. But come up with a new accessory or adapt an existing one and you're on your way.

I'll give you an example of how to become rich by creating "must have" accessories that appeal to the amateur. Plain white wooden tee pegs (see *Tees*) can be purchased for about £2.50 to £3.00 per hundred from most sporting goods shops. But paint a coloured stripe around the middle of a plain white tee peg, call it a "teeing system" which will make sure the ball is always tee'd up to the same height, sell these at £5.00 for 50 and you're on your way to your first million. Don't try this idea because it has already been done (sadly, not by me).

I would like to say that I'm immune to the blandishments of the accessory manufacturers, but I'm afraid I'm as much of a sucker as everyone else.

Aids

Golfing aids are any item of equipment that assists the golfer in deciding what shot to play, which club to use, how hard to hit the ball and in which direction. Because these can have a direct impact on the player's performance on the course, they are governed by the rules of the game.

However, the rules appear to be somewhat arbitrary.

For example, under Rule 4.3a(1) you are not allowed to use any device that will tell you the wind speed or direction. But under rule 4.3a(2) you are allowed to use a distance measuring device to judge how far it is to the hole, to a bunker or to a lake.

Now, to my mind, knowing how far it is to the hole is just as important as knowing which direction the wind is from and how strong it is. Both will affect the choice of club and shot to be played.

But the rules of golf are quite clear - one is allowed and the other isn't.

There are a range of devices that allow amateurs to establish the distance to the hole, most of which use GPS technology, so there isn't so much of an opportunity to become rich in coming up with new golfing aids. The device I currently own allows me to see distances to bunkers and lakes, which is very useful information. I did think of developing a device that offered recorded advice on how to play a particular hole from the club professional (see *Pro*), but the R&A got there before me, because that would count as "seeking advice" which isn't allowed under rule 10.2a.

There are two schools of thought amongst amateurs with regards to the use of the golfing aids that are permitted. Some amateurs regard the use of such aids as being unnecessary. The Mk 1 eyeball and a bit of grass tossed into the air has served them well all their lives and they will continue to rely on that, thank you very much. For all the rest, the must have gift for Christmas is always going to be the latest golfing aid. I am firmly in the latter group.

I have been known to stand beside the 100 yard marker (see *Distance markers*) on the fairway and consult my GPS device to establish that it is exactly 100 yards to the centre of the green (though not necessarily – see *Distance markers*).

I know my own course like the back of my hand, having played so many rounds of golf there that my footprints are visible permanently, like the fossilised prints of a dinosaur. But when I play unfamiliar courses my device is a boon.

Air shot

An air shot is a common thing for those just starting the game. The novice takes an almighty swing at the ball and misses completely, often going off balance and falling over, much to the amusement of their partners.

While more experienced amateurs don't experience these very often, they aren't unknown. On some occasions, it has been known for the amateur's golf club to fly out of their hand during an air shot, threatening the safety of all around. On one memorable occasion, my club landed on the roof of a house close to the edge of the course (I did manage to get it back).

In January 2020, while still compiling this book, I asked my partners for the day whether or not I should include this term.

"Hardly necessary", two of them replied.

"I can't remember the last time I had an air shot." one of them added.

Within ten minutes, the partner who couldn't remember his last air shot had just performed one and another partner had one before the end of the round.

"You're going to put that in your book now, aren't you?" One of them said.

"Yes." said I.

It isn't an uncommon phenomenon in golf, for golfers to suffer whatever ill is under discussion. It only needs the word "shank" (see *Shank*) to be whispered somewhere on the course for golfers several holes away to start doing it. I suspect that the golfing Gods are listening and laughing over inflicting these indignities on the amateur and by saying the word they are taking it as a suggestion for something to inflict upon us. Or we could just be very suggestible.

In the USA the air shot is known as a "whiff".

Albatross

A large, white, sea going bird with a yellow beak. Lives on a diet of fish. Usually found in the Antarctic Ocean. Has been known to stay aloft for up to 2 years. Sleeps while in the air. This is a feat that I can't emulate even with the benefit of an aeroplane (I don't trust the pilot, so I have to stay awake to keep an eye on him/her).

Rumours of albatrosses near golf courses frequented by amateurs abound, but just like pilots, you should never place your trust in them. They are probably just big seagulls.

Also the golfing term for scoring three under par (see *Par*). That equates to a hole-in-one (see *Hole-in-one*) on a par 4 hole or a score of two on a par 5. While this is theoretically possible, especially on a golf course with short par 4 or par 5 holes, the reality is somewhat more difficult.

Gene Sarazan was the first professional golfer to score an albatross, on the par five 15th hole at the 1935 Masters at Augusta (see *Augusta*). The most recent one was scored by Nicholas Thompson at the par five 11th hole at the Grayhawk Golf Club in Scottsdale, Arizona, in 2007. He then scored a hole-in-one at the par three 12th hole, a highly improbable back to back combination. Anyone who placed a bet on the two events occurring in that way is now probably the owner of the Crown Jewels.

In terms of probability, an albatross is a less likely achievement than a hole-in-one. I have had a hole-in-one but never an albatross, so I suspect this to be true. The odds against scoring an albatross are 12,700 to 1, slightly longer than the odds for an amateur to make a hole-in-one but considerably longer than the odds for a pro to achieve the same feat.

The origin of the appellation "albatross" may be from an amateur who claimed the feat in 1934 at the Nishak course in India, on the par 5 9th hole. His name was J G Ridland and he is supposed to have suggested the name, to maintain the theme set by "birdie" and "eagle" (see both terms below). However, this story is somewhat undermined by at least nine prior published references to the term being used in golf, dating back to 1929. Before the recognised use of the term "albatross", the feat had been known as a "double eagle".

It is theorised that the arrival of steel shafted clubs around the late 1920s, to replace wooden shafts, increased the frequency with which albatrosses were scored, as the steel shafts increased the distance that could be achieved. Ridland himself was using a new set of steel shafted clubs.

The most recent reference I can find to an amateur scoring an albatross is of Will Reeves, a High School golfer in the USA. He achieved this feat at the par five 5th hole at the Prairie Falls Golf

Club in Post Falls, Idaho, in 2019. He was playing in the Washington Junior Golf Association District 5 Sub-District tournament (snappy name, huh?). He also scored birdies on two other holes on the same 9. Sadly, just two holes after scoring his albatross, Reeves scored 21 on the par four 7th hole. Despite a respectable score for the back 9 (see *Front 9* and *Back 9*), he finished with a gross (see *Gross* and *Nett*) score of 92. I think that all amateurs can relate to the highs and lows of that round.

Amateur status

You would think that the definition of amateur status would be quite a simple matter. Just don't take money for winning. But it isn't that easy. Amateur status also applies to the winning of prizes.

Basically, an amateur golfer may not play golf for a cash prize. But as any amateur will tell you, playing for money is quite a normal occurrence for amateurs. This is because the money isn't offered as a prize for the competition. It is run as a sweepstake instead. It is essentially a low stakes bet (see *Gambling*) played for amongst the players, which the participants are free to opt out of. If you come first in the competition and you have opted out of the "sweep" you get only the glory of winning and whatever the official prize is. As some minor or "fun" club competitions don't offer an official prize, you end up returning home empty handed.

When it comes to non-cash prizes, an amateur cannot win anything with a value of more than £500. That is actually quite a generous amount. In real terms it only excludes certain "high end" brands of golf clubs. This rule is waived for the winning of a hole-in-one prize.

An amateur may win a voucher with a set value attached, such as a meal for two, golf equipment, a hotel break or even a holiday, but the £500 limit still applies and the voucher can't be convertible to cash. Interestingly, though, a voucher may be used to offset some cash spending within the club that awarded it, such as a bar bill, competition entry fees or even annual membership. I can't help but think that the clubs exercised a bit of self-interest when they came up with that one.

It is quite common for the sponsors of pro-am (see *Pro-Am*) tournaments to offer a prize as valuable as a car for anyone who scores a hole-in-one on a specific hole. Because of the rules of amateur status, the "am" part of the partnership couldn't claim their prize unless they were willing to turn professional on the spot. This has since changed and the lucky amateur can now accept the car. If the prize is in cash, they can accept the prize if they are willing to forfeit their amateur status. Once forfeited, the golfer can't compete as an amateur again for two years. For a big enough wad of cash, I think I'd make the sacrifice. After all, I would still be able to play golf, I just wouldn't be able to enter amateur competitions.

An amateur can play in a competition or tournament where there is a cash prize, but they must first waive their right (in writing) to the prize money.

If you think the above explanations are as clear as mud, you are in good company. The rules of amateur status have confused golfers for many years and more than one amateur has fallen foul of them, especially in relation to accepting high value non-cash prizes. What is worse is that tournament or competition organisers have also transgressed by offering prizes that break the rules, which has left the amateur thinking they had done nothing wrong.

ASHES (SCATTERING OF)

It is quite common for a member to request that their ashes are scattered at the golf club where they were a member, when they go to that great golf course in the sky. Even if the golfer doesn't request it, their family often does. Technically this is "fly tipping".

If the deceased member's family wish to scatter the ashes of a loved one they must (a) have the club's permission and (b) only scatter the ashes in the area designated by the golf club management. This is almost never where the family want them to be scattered.

Augusta

There are two temples to the Gods of golf. One is St Andrews, discussed later and the other, in my humble opinion, is the Augusta National, home to The Masters tournament. I won't get into an argument about which is the better course. They are different in style and character, so it would be like comparing apples with oranges.

Founded in 1932 by Bobby Jones (a well-known and very wealthy amateur golfer) and Clifford Roberts (another wealthy amateur, but not so well known), the club has had its share of controversy, especially with regards to race and feminism. Co-founder Roberts was quoted as saying "As long as I'm alive, all the golfers will be white and all the caddies will be black."

It wasn't until 1975 that a person of colour, Lee Elder, was permitted to participate in the Masters. Women weren't allowed to become members of the club until 2012.

Sadly, mere mortals such as the average amateur will never be able to become members at this wonderful course. They have about 300 members at any one time, but you have to be invited to join. Unsurprisingly, it isn't what you know about golf that is the deciding factor when it comes to membership, it is much more about who you know (and how much money you have). The current membership is a "who's who" of the rich and famous: Warren Buffet, Bill Gates, Jack Nicklaus and a host of business leaders sprinkled with the odd politician and sports star. Condoleezza Rice, Secretary of State to President George W Bush, is the most prominent female member and person of colour.

The club is very reticent when it comes to discussing money, but it is believed that to become a member costs between $10,000 and $30,000, with annual fees of about $10,000.

The establishment of The Masters at Augusta was a consequence of the Great Depression. With money tight even amongst the wealthy, the club was struggling to keep afloat. The establishment of a tournament to attract paying spectators was one of the measures taken to boost income. The first Masters tournament took place in

1934. Bobby Jones, one of the co-founders of the club and a leading name in amateur golf, was coaxed out of retirement to headline the tournament.

Famously each hole on the course is named after a different flower or shrub. This is a reference to the prior use of the land as a plant nursery. Each hole is now planted with a bush or shrub with the corresponding name to the hole. However, most of the flowers seen on TV at the Masters have been reared specifically for the Masters and planted just for the event, as so many species are un-cooperative and don't flower in April in Georgia.

Over the years, the course has been made longer and therefore a much more challenging test of the golfer's skill. In 1940 it was 6,800 yards but is now 7,475 yards in length. Considering that the course where I play is a modest 6,085 yards (off the championship tees) that is quite a step up for an amateur to make. Just thinking about the distance I would have to walk to complete a round* makes me tired.

For most amateurs, playing the Augusta National will only ever be a dream. Members can invite guests to play the course, but amateurs can't just play as a visitor. There is a faint possibility of playing if you join the Augusta Country Club instead. Augusta National members in need of a fourth player have been known to ring the country club to invite someone to make up the numbers. You can also play by becoming the British (or American) Amateur Champion. They get an automatic invite to play in The Masters.

* Amateur golfers never proceed in straight lines around a golf course, so their walking distance has to be calculated from a series of zigzags. This is sometimes referred to as playing "regimental" or "military" golf, because you go left, right, left, right. The length of the golf course as stated on the scorecard (see *Scorecard*) bears no relation to the distance the amateur will actually cover during the round.

Awayday

The one disadvantage of being a member of a golf club is the lack of variety. You play the same course round after round, week after week, year after year. While each stroke is different and is made from a different place, meaning that each round is different, the scenery never varies, other than with the changing weather or season. For this reason amateurs often go on awaydays.

This is not a feature of professional golf, of course, because every tournament is an awayday for most professionals. Only if one of the tournaments is played on their "home" course will any professional play the same course twice in a year, other than through choice.

An awayday is an organised visit to another golf course. In most cases the course to be played will be within an hour's travelling distance. If it is any further away then they start to involve hotels and become "tours" rather than awaydays. Both are discussed here.

The awayday is supposed to be a fun event. It may involve a competition (golfers are often very competitive) but they don't have to. They will also often involve food and drink either before or after the competition.

Just choosing which course to visit can be a problem. Asking twenty golfers which course they want to play for the next awayday, will result in twenty different answers. The organiser then has to choose one, which means that nineteen people will feel slighted because their choice wasn't the one selected. When I organise awaydays, I choose the course I want to play. It actually causes less offence.

Golf clubs don't like their members going on awaydays because they take their money to other courses and spend it in the bar or dining room there. On the other hand, golf clubs love hosting awaydays for the same reason. Fortunately, we still live in a free country, so the club management can't actually stop their members organising awaydays, providing they don't use club funds to do it.

As mentioned above, when hotels become involved, in order to accommodate overnight stays, the awayday becomes a tour. It usually then involves two rounds of golf, one on the day of arrival and one on the day of departure, sometimes at the same course but sometimes at another course in the area, or which is passed en-route. Tours can last much longer, perhaps involving a full week in Spain, Portugal, or Florida in the winter.

As the golf itself is limited to daylight, the evenings are the thing to be careful of, large quantities of alcohol can be consumed, and behaviour, so restrained at home, sometimes becomes a little extreme for golfers who aren't used to such freedom without their spouse being present. That comment isn't just restricted to male golfers. As may be imagined, the golf played on the second day (and subsequent days) of a tour is usually of a lower standard to that played on the first day.

Tours usually generate stories, some of which the amateur would rather didn't reach the ears of their spouse. The saying "What happens in Vegas, stays in Vegas" doesn't always apply. So, on tour, remember that stories travel and often grow in the telling. My own behaviour on tour is always impeccable and I am the epitome of sobriety. And I'm not saying that just because my wife will probably read this book.

I have one story I can tell about tours, because it didn't involve one that I went on. I was at home one evening when the telephone rang. I answered it to hear the voice of an Irish female. "Do you know Helmut, by any chance?" the lady asked (name chosen to provide anonymity, but he wasn't German).

It turned out that Helmut had met the lady while on a golfing tour to Ireland some weeks earlier. She had tracked me down because Helmut had said he came from my village and at that time my name and phone number appeared on the website for our village golf society (see *Societies*) as the person to whom inquiries should be directed. Anyway, the lady went on to say that she had something important to tell Helmut and could I pass on a message? Helmut wasn't actually a member of our society but he had been at one time, so I was acquainted with him and saw him just a few days later. I dutifully passed on the message, but it was noticeable that he became very anxious to put distance between himself and me and I don't normally have that effect on people. He wasn't even with his wife at the time.

So beware, in this day and age, no one is impossible to track down.

B is For

Back spin

One of golf's holy grails. Imparting back spin onto a ball (see *ball*) gives it "lift", so it stays in the air for longer and therefore travels a greater distance. However, it also brings the ball to a rapid stop when it lands, as the back spin "grips" the grass and prevents the ball from bouncing forward.

It is through the use of backspin that professional golfers are able to get such accuracy with their shots, stopping them in the right place seemingly at will.

The ability of an amateur to harness back spin usually ensures their handicap (see *Handicap*) is in single figures.

The opposite of back spin is "top spin". Top spin usually makes a ball nose dive towards the ground after being hit and will also prevent the ball stopping where the golfer wants it to stop.

Side spin is what causes the ball to slice or hook, ie turn rapidly off-line from the intended direction of travel. Sometimes it can't be detected until the ball hits the ground, when the ball can sometimes turn at right angles to the intended direction as the spin grips the ground. Sidespin is caused by hitting across the ball (swinging the club from inside the line to outside, or outside the line to inside) rather than behind it, which is usually a side effect of trying to hit the ball too hard.

Back swing

That part of a golf shot that draws the club head away from the ball in preparation for it to strike the ball and send it on its way. Getting the back swing right is one of the fundamental parts of making a good shot.

Ball

You would think that something as simple as a ball wouldn't require much discussion, but there are 6 separate rules of golf covering balls, which spread over 18 pages of the player's edition of the RoG.

And that is before we get into discussions about which ball is best.

First of all, a golf ball has to conform to the rules laid down for it under the general heading of "equipment". That isn't too much of a problem for the amateur. If you are buying a golf ball from a reputable source then it is going to conform. But there are fakes and counterfeits on the market, so buyer beware. A modern golf ball should measure one point six eight inches in diameter (1.68 in, or 42.67 mm).

There are even "trick" balls available, sold as novelties. If one of your partners ever insists that you use a ball that they have given you, don't be surprised if it explodes into a cloud of powder when you strike it, or it takes on a rather eccentric flight path (that is to say more eccentric than the way you normally hit a ball).

All games that involve a ball have some rule to say what a legal ball is, so golf isn't unusual in that respect. It is what happens when you actually play the ball that generates all those rules. Most of these are covered elsewhere in this book.

Not all golf balls are equal and some heated conversations have been known to take place between golfers on the subject of which ball is best. This is compounded by the fact that many professionals are sponsored to use a particular brand of golf ball. Given that a player of the calibre of Tiger Woods (the real one, not my mate Tim) could probably get a half decent round of golf out of a ball bearing covered in sausage meat, it becomes difficult for the amateur to decide which brand of ball to use.

Many golfers swear by the "feel" of a golf ball; that different brands of ball "feel" different when they play their stroke. I have been playing this game for many years and I wouldn't recognise the "feel" of a ball if it was giving me an all over body massage. I suspect that the whole concept of "feel" was made up by a marketing executive and was spread by gullible golf journalists.

Ball manufacturers play on the amateur's insecurity by selling several different types of ball. These are distinguished by the printing on the ball alongside the brand name. Phrases like "tour pro", "distance", "tour trajectory" etc. My own favourite is "marathon distance" which suggests the golfer should be able to hit it over 26 miles. I am convinced that these words are meaningless and are there simply to justify a price difference between that ball and another one made by the same manufacturer but at a lower price.

There is even one manufacturer that holds golf "clinics" at golf clubs where amateurs can try out their different types of ball under the watchful eye of a pro, who will recommend which of their wide range of balls to use. I may be an old cynic (**Editor's note**: Yes, you are) but I wonder how many players are recommended to use the more expensive balls in the range.

The difference in price in some balls is quite remarkable. The Dixon Fire ball is sold at $75 dollars per dozen. I think my golf balls are expensive if I pay £10 (about $15) per dozen.

The cheapest way to get expensive golf balls is to either find them (they get lost just as easily as cheap balls (see *Lost Ball*)) or to buy reconditioned ones. All those practice balls that the pros play on the driving ranges before each round are re-packaged and sold off, generally on the internet but also in some pro shops (see *Pro Shop*) and specialist golf shops.

Most pros replace their golf ball after a few holes, with some even using a new ball on every hole. I have some golf balls in my bag that have survived over a hundred holes of golf and are starting to change shape from spheres to cubes. That is another difference between the pro and the amateur. Of course, not all amateurs are as parsimonious as me, but even so, it is unusual for an amateur to replace their ball during a round of golf unless it becomes damaged - or lost, which is more likely.

Just for the record, it is against the rules of golf to replace the ball in "mid hole" unless damage has been identified. The ball may only be replaced before teeing off.

Rule 6.3 of golf states that you must put an identifying mark on your ball before you start play. With all golf balls looking very similar (except, occasionally, for their colour) it is easy to confuse one ball for another and to play the wrong ball, which will incur a penalty (see *Penalty*).

However, it is key to this rule that you all use different markings on your ball. Many people use lines, dots, x's etc, so sometimes putting a mark on your ball serves no real purpose. On at least one occasion I have discovered half way through a round that the mark I used for my ball was so similar to the mark one of my partners was using that we may, inadvertently, have played each other's balls at some time or another, which could lead to disqualification (see *DQ*).

I now use a very distinctive identification mark for my golf balls which, to the best of my knowledge, no other member of my club uses.

However, that didn't end the problem of misidentification. Like most amateurs, on occasion I have lost balls, but just like money that is lost, a lost ball can be found subsequently. Approaching the 18th green towards the end of a competition I was helping a partner to look for his ball, when I found one in the rough in about the right place for it to be his. I picked it up to identify it and saw that it had my distinctive marking on it. Naturally I assumed that the ball was mine, one I had previously lost and I could now rejoice at the return of a prodigal ball.

I commented on the fact, only to be told by my partner that it was his ball, which he had been playing since he had lost a ball on a previous hole. During the discussion it emerged that he had found the ball elsewhere on the course during another round. Fortunately, I was allowed to replace the ball where I had found it and he played his shot. Unfortunately, I suffered a one shot penalty because I hadn't marked the spot where I had found the ball before lifting it to identify it (Rule 7.3).

There is an old joke in golf (skip over if you've heard it) that relates to the marking of golf balls.

A seasoned amateur is explaining to a "newbie" golfer the need to mark their ball before tee-off.

"If you can't see where your ball ends up, it isn't easy to know if the ball you find is yours or someone else's" The seasoned amateur explained.

"Why?" asks the newbie. "Surely we all know which ball we're using?"

"It's not that easy," says the amateur. "Say I'm using a Titelist ball and you're also using a Titelist ball and they end up side by side. We won't know which is yours and which is mine."

"Tell you what," says the newbie. "I'll switch to a Srixon."

I said it was an old joke, I didn't say it was a funny one.

One important thing to remember about a golf ball is that it has a very hard exterior and once it has been hit it is travelling very fast. When it leaves the club face it could be travelling at 150 mph and even when it hits the ground it will still be doing 45 mph. This means that it packs a punch if it hits you - or anyone else. A golf ball can kill and I can testify to how much it hurts even if it just hits you on the arm. I had "Pinnacle" printed on my skin in "mirror writing" for days after being struck by a golf ball and the bruising took weeks to fade. So it is best to make sure you are in a safe position when those around you are playing their shots.

Balls - a short history

The bit of golf equipment that has gone through the most changes over time are golf balls. You can pick up a golf club made over two hundred years ago and it will still be familiar in most respects. Other than with a driver (see *Driver*), most golfers will be able to get a similar sort of distance with their stroke with the antique. But that isn't true for the golf ball. Other than being round, they are very different to those used in earlier times.

No one is sure quite when the first golf ball was hit. The game probably developed from shepherds hitting pebbles, pine cones or clumps of wool with their crooks as a way of passing a boring day. So we don't know when the first golf ball was made, but we do have some idea of what it was made of.

Actually, we do have some idea when the first golf ball was made, in terms of which century, but we can't narrow that down to a year or even a decade. In the 14th century balls started to be made of wood, usually beech. Each one was hand craved by a carpenter, which made them expensive. So it is understandable why golfers might pay a "forecaddie" (see *Fore*) to stand at the side of a fairway to keep a lookout for the ball and reduce the risk of it being lost. Even the best carpenters couldn't carve a perfect spherical ball, so the flight would have been unpredictable, to say the least.

The wooden ball remained in service until around the 17th century, when someone came up the idea of stuffing feathers into a leather pouch. This became known as the "feathery". It produced a much lighter ball, which could be propelled further, but the shape was still a problem, as it's just as hard to sew a perfect sphere as it is to carve one. With lighter balls came the possibility of using golf clubs with a more flexible shaft, which introduced "whip" into the equation. The solid wooden ball was more likely to break a club with a thin shaft. There is a game called "street golf" which uses "hacky sacks" instead of golf balls and these are basically modern day featheries.

In the middle of the 18th century we get the "guttie", invented by Robert Adams Patterson. The sap of the Malaysian Sapodilla tree could be heated and put into a mould to make a round ball. Technically the sap is known as gutta percha and refers to the latex like substance produced by the trees. Some golf balls made with the material were known as gutta perchas. While some people think this is the same material as rubber, it isn't. It is more closely related to chiclé, the basic ingredient for natural chewing gum. This ball had the advantage that if it started to go out of shape it could be re-heated and re-moulded. This was the first ball that could be mass produced, which fitted well with the Victorian age of mass manufacturing and brought about a considerable reduction in the price of golf balls.

One special discovery was made with the guttie. A nicked and bashed about guttie flew further and straighter than a perfectly smooth one. It seemed that those nicks and dents stabilised the ball in flight. What was being observed was the basics of aerodynamics, though golfers didn't know that at the time.

From that discovery onwards, golf ball manufacturers started to mould or carve their balls with textured surfaces to make them behave better in flight. These came in various styles and patterns, with each manufacturer claiming that their pattern was the most effective. I'm guessing here, but I think that was probably the origin of the differential marketing of golf balls based on their flight characteristics, which I touched on above.

The next innovation came about equally by accident. A visitor to the B F Goodrich rubber factory, by the name of Coburn Haskell, started winding rubber bands (a B F Goodrich product) into a ball while he waited for his golfing partner to finish work. He bounced the ball on the floor and discovered that the potential energy that he had created in the bundle of rubber bands was released in the form of increased bounce. Haskell and his golf partner, Bertram Work, covered the ball in the sap of the Balata tree (a material that substitutes for rubber) and the guttie ball became a thing of the past.

While pimples and other surface patterns were still in use, some sharp-eyed golfer (unknown) observed that a ball flew better if it was covered with dimples, rather than protrusions. This was around 1900. This progressed to the ball that we know today, which has a hard plastic exterior wrapped around a synthetic interior and a dimpled surface. The big advantage of dimples over pimples was that back spin could be put onto the ball, which will make it stop pretty much where it lands. This is something that the pros are able to exploit but which the amateur golfer still struggles with - but we all do it occasionally and it's great when it happens on a shot into the green, leaving the ball inches from the hole rather than bouncing through the green to roll off the far side.

Only the nature of the materials themselves has changed since 1900 as new ones have been invented. Golf ball design is now no longer a matter of observation and accidental discovery, it is a matter of serious scientific research. With the global golf ball market worth about $1.1 billion a year, it is far too serious a business to be left in the hands of the artisan and the enthusiastic amateur.

Ball Marker

A small metal or plastic token that is used to mark the position of the ball when it is lifted, as is allowed when on the green. Because they are quite small, it is easy to lose and partners get very annoyed when you delay the game as you empty your pocket trying to find yours.

Many golf clubs sell ball markers with their club name or logo on them. If you are the sort of person who likes to collect things, there is a new hobby waiting for you right there. You can also buy personalised ball markers through some golfing websites. Matching ball markers and pitch mark repairers (see *Pitch mark*) are often handed out as mementos of important competitions, such as Captain's Day.

See also "accessories".

Benches

You can tell whether a golf club is mainly a "young person's club" or an "old person's club" by the number of benches there are around the course. This isn't because older golfers need to sit down more (although they do), it is because more older members die and their loved ones donate benches in their memory, complete with a commemorative metal plate telling users who they were.

The owner of our club decided that there was a risk of the course having too many benches, so he now has just two designated for the purposes of memorials; one for the ladies and one for the men. The deceased's loved ones are able to request that a commemorative plate (which they pay for) is attached to the relevant bench in memory of their loved one.

Birdie

Even amateur golfers have been known to score the odd birdie or two. The term means scoring one stroke under par for the hole. Even your humble author has scored birdies and on one notable occasion scored back-to-back birdies on successive holes.

The origins of the term are in American slang where, at one time, to refer to something as "bird" meant that it was good, much as the youth of today use the word "sick" in the same way.

The Country Club in Atlantic City, New Jersey, claims the first use of the term in relation to golf. A conversation between two golfers, A B Smith and his friend George A Crump, was reported in a 1962 issue of US Greenkeeper magazine, in which Smith claimed he said "that was a bird of a shot" when his ball rolled to within inches of the hole on his second shot of a par 4, allowing him to complete the hole in 3. The club itself dates that conversation to 1903.

The first recorded written use of the term appeared in a 1911 edition of McLean Magazine, when a golf shot of two hundred and fifteen yards straight down the fairway was described as "bird".

Bite

A word shouted by a golfer who has just hit a "hot" shot out of a bunker (see *Bunker*) to send the ball flying across the green. He is essentially asking he ball to develop back spin (see *Back spin*) in order to stop the ball on the green.

It rarely, if ever, happens.

Bogey and double bogey (and more)

A bogey is by far the most common score for the amateur as it means a score of one over par. With the amateur's handicap allowance it means that they have usually scored a par on the hole and are rewarded as such. Players with a handicap in excess of 18 can score a double bogey and still be rewarded with a par for the hole (see *Stroke Index* for a lengthier explanation of this).

However, the original use of the term bogey was actually to mean par and the term par itself entered the language later.

Back in the 1800s the Secretary of the Coventry Golf Club, Mr Hugh Rotherham, came up with the idea of standardising the number of shots that the holes on a course should be played in, depending on the length of the holes and the number of holes on the course. This he called "the ground score".

The system was adopted at Great Yarmouth Golf Club and used in "match play" (see *Match play*) competitions. During one such competition, one spectator, Mr C A Wellman (possibly a Major) is alleged to have said "Here comes the bogey man", referring to another member's prowess in achieving the "ground score". The use of the term "bogey man" probably relates to a popular music hall song of the era, called "Hush! Hush! Hush! Here Comes The Bogey Man." which had nothing to do with golf.

From there and at other nearby courses, achieving the ground score for a hole became known as a bogey.

Other possibilities for the use of the term bogey or bogie is the meaning of the term in relation to goblins. Certainly in Scotland, that bastion of golf, the word bogie meant a goblin.

Golfers of the day came to compare themselves with what "Mr Bogey" would score on a hole, introducing it to a wider audience. It is certain that it was in use in 1892 when The Field magazine referred to the introduction of a "Bogey tournament" when fourteen couples entered but "the bogey defeated them all". Presumably that meant that none of the entrants achieved the requisite score.

Also in 1892, at the United Services Club in Gosport, Hampshire, all members were considered to have a military rank (even if they didn't) so nobody could play against Mr Bogey. Instead they played against Colonel Bogey, which gave rise to the term being used as the title of a piece of music composed in 1914 and gaining worldwide fame as the theme tune for the film "Bridge On The River Kwai".

So, when did "bogey" come to mean one over par, rather than par itself?

The term "par" had first appeared in 1870 and when American golfers first started to play in England they found some of our courses, limited by length, easier than their own longer courses back home. This meant that they frequently scored less than the bogey score. They therefore regarded bogey as being one over par. I am unable to find a date for this change, but it was probably after the First World War. With golf being reported on the radio in the USA and featuring in cinema newsreels in the UK, the American terminology stuck and the British bogey earned a new meaning.

No one has ever seen it necessary to invent a term to describe double bogeys and higher because professionals score them so rarely. However, for us amateurs, they are a common occurrence. Indeed, with recent changes to the handicapping system it is expected that triple bogeys are par for some golfers.

May I suggest the introduction of the term "dammit" for the double bogey and the "sugar" for a triple bogey. Much stronger language is frequently used to describe these scores, but we want to encourage children to play the game of golf so the use of swear words shouldn't be within hearing range of their more delicate ears.

If, at some point in the future, you should hear those two terms being used at the golf club, please make sure to reference this book. Even if I have gone on to that great golf course in the sky, my children will still be receiving my royalties (**Publisher's note**: and so will I).

Buggy

A small powered car, usually a two-seater, used by golfers to take them and their golf clubs around the golf course in relative comfort. Most of them are rented out by the golf club, but it isn't unknown for golfers to own their own. A single seat version can be purchased for around £1,200.

There are two types of buggy, those with a two-stroke engine and those that are battery powered. The two-stroke engined versions smell appallingly, while the battery powered ones often run out of "juice" part way through the round if they haven't had a chance to re-charge fully since last being used; but at least they don't smell.

I don't like using a buggy much. Playing golf to the standard at which I play, getting exercise is one of the few justifications I have for playing the game at all. However, in 2019, I suffered from knee problems and the use of a buggy was the only way I was able to play the game.

But I find that I play worse (if that is possible) when using a buggy. I suspect that my muscles never warm up enough, so I'm not able to "get my swing going" as we golfers say.

In some hotter countries, taking a golf buggy is mandatory, because of the risk of over-heating if you try to walk. Some golfers like to take a buggy because there is a basket behind the seat large enough to store beer.

It is a general rule of golf clubs that the golfers using buggies are those who would benefit most from walking (excluding those suffering from knee problems, of course).

Golfers must beware, because buggies can bite. Please learn from these cautionary tales.

While golfing in Bermuda (long story) our 4 ball group (see *Four ball*) was using two buggies to speed up the round. The driver of the other buggy decided to try to drive across the steep slope that led to the next green, rather than down it and rolled the buggy. Fortunately neither he nor his partner (who was also his wife) were injured, but both they and their beer stocks were severely shaken, not stirred.

Back in the UK, at a neighbouring golf club, the driver of a buggy had to navigate around the edge of a water hazard. He got too close and found himself driving around the bank, instead of on the flat and he rolled his buggy into the water, which was quite deep. Again, fortune favoured him and his partner, but the water soaked them and all their kit and shorted out the buggy's electrical systems.

Finally, a friend was waiting in a queue beside the tee of a par 3 hole which has a bad reputation for being slow to play. A 4 ball group from a golf society (see *Societies*) approached from the previous hole, travelling in two buggies, One of the buggy drivers decided to show off his driving skills by approaching the queue at full speed then slamming on the brakes at the last moment, to bring the buggy to a sliding stop. He mistimed it and drove into my friend, seriously damaging his knee. He was unable to play golf for several weeks.

A buggy is useful if you want to carry some refreshment.

Bunkers

A bunker is a large hole in the ground which has been partially refilled with sand. The front "face" of the bunker is usually far higher than the rear. This allows the ball to roll in easily but makes it much harder to get the ball out again. They are one of two types of hazard covered by the RoG (see *Hazard*).

There are sadistic golf course designers who relish the chance to put a huge and/or very deep bunker on a golf course. These people are evil.

Bunkers are also things that people fail to rake when they have used them. I blame the pros for that.

The armchair golfer sees the pro go into the bunker, sees the pro play his shot out of the bunker and sees the pro getting out of the bunker and handing their club to their caddy before walking on to where their ball has landed. They don't see the pro rake the bunker, so the armchair golfer gets it into their head that there is no need to rake the bunker.

What they don't see is the caddy, or a greenkeeper, go into the bunker straight after the pro has left it and rake it for him, because the TV cameras have already moved on. The directors of TV coverage could do a lot worse than to show the bunkers being raked after use.

Rant over, please continue reading.

It is said that professional golfers prefer to play out of a bunker than play out of the rough. I don't believe that. For the amateur to land in a bunker, it can often mean the end of their round in terms of any reasonable score. Even those amateurs who are good at getting out of bunkers don't like being in them.

You may be starting to think that I don't like bunkers. You would be right. Given the choice of being in a bunker or being in water (see *Water*), I'll take the water every time. At least you know where you are with water. It may cost you a penalty shot to claim relief (see *Relief*), but at least you won't end up taking ten shots to get out (but see later, when I tell a particularly harrowing story about water).

I once spent so long getting out of a bunker that my partners started calling me Adolf (younger readers may not get that joke).

There are basically two types of bunker, the fairway bunker and the greenside bunker.

The fairway bunker is there to trap the golfer off the tee (or on their second shot if the hole is a par 5). It is strategically positioned so as to capture the boldest shots. Under normal circumstances the average amateur shouldn't have to worry about fairway bunkers as their tee shots will rarely travel that far. Their problem is getting past the bunker with their next shot. When you know that a bunker is there, you are mentally dragged towards it.

Finding yourself in fairway bunkers is bound to cost a shot, because the front lip prevents the amateur from playing the sort of shot that will gain them any distance. To get over the front lip of the bunker calls for the use of a "lofted" club (one that lifts the ball up rather than driving it forward) so distance is sacrificed.

Fairway bunkers are also usually the largest. Some are so large that they resemble deserts. I have been known to be at the rearward end of one of these big beggars and still haven't reached the front two shots later.

The second type of bunker is the green-side bunker. These are much harder to avoid as they are positioned specifically to make it harder for the golfer to reach the green. A shot that is slightly wayward is placed in jeopardy by the positioning of these bunkers. Generally speaking, these are positioned to the sides of the green, but there are some golf course designers (or 'bastards', as I call them) who position them so that a frontal approach is also made more difficult. If the green slopes downwards towards the rear, then it can almost be guaranteed that the bastard, sorry the designer, will put a bunker at the back of the green as well.

So, what is it that makes playing out of a bunker so difficult. In a word: sand.

Sand is soft, so that if your club hits it, it drains a lot of power from the shot, so the ball doesn't get enough velocity and it ends up not reaching the front lip. If you hit the ball with the edge of the club, which drives the ball much harder, you get no elevation and so, again, the ball hits the front face of the bunker instead of escaping.

All this is made so much harder when it has rained. The water drains out of the bunker through the bottom, but in doing so, it packs the sand tight, turning it into something akin to concrete. If your ball is lying on that when you play your shot, the club face is likely to ricochet off the bottom and catch the ball halfway up, with the consequences noted earlier.

The worst shot to have to play from a bunker, however, is the "poached egg". This is when the ball has dropped in from a great height, half burying itself in sand and giving it the look of a half cooked poached egg. It is very difficult to get the face of the club to penetrate the sand deep enough to lift the ball out of the sand and into the air.

Then the R&A added their tuppence by stating that you can't ground your club in a hazard, which means you can't rest your club behind the ball as you prepare to take your shot. This means that as you set up for your stroke, the face of the club is hovering in the air. This, in itself, tends to force poor shots.

I would like to say that it is only high handicap amateurs that suffer in bunkers, but I have also seen low handicappers suffering.

The feelings of amateurs about bunkers can be summed up by an old TV advert for a brand of cigar, first shown in 1980, which captures the frustrations perfectly. The theme of a series of ads for this cigar was that, no matter how bad things got, smoking this particular brand made things feel better, even if they weren't actually better.

The scene for the ad in question was a golf course. We never see the golfer, because he is deep within a bunker. We see the top of his golf club as he takes his back swing, we hear his grunt of exertion as he makes his stroke, we see a spray of sand emerge from the bunker, but no ball. This is repeated several times, before we hear the striking of a match, we see a puff of cigar smoke appearing above the lip of the bunker, followed by a contended sigh and an extract of

Bach's "Air on A G String" playing (the theme music for all the adverts).

Being a reformed smoker I now hate smoking but, trapped in a bunker, I have often felt the need to re-start.

C is For

Caddy

A box or tin used for the storage of tea, or tees. Unless you are a millionaire that's all you need to know about caddies.

Actually, if you ever play golf in Thailand (and other countries in South East Asia possibly), I had better tell you a bit more.

At many golf clubs in Thailand, it is mandatory to take a caddy with you on the course. I think it is probably an employment scheme and helpful to the local economy. These caddies are usually female and, at the risk of sounding sexist, pretty. There are three things you need to know about these caddies:

1. Because they are pretty, it is easy to become distracted from your golf.
2. The caddies are mainly self-employed, so it will be up to you to pay them but check in the clubhouse when you pay your green fee. Feel free to add a tip.
3. The caddies are there to meet only your golfing needs. If you expect anything else, you are in the wrong sort of club.

Actually, at some clubs you may have a caddy (probably a volunteer) for some of their bigger competitions. This being the case, it is useful to know that they are specifically mentioned in the RoG with regard to what they are and aren't allowed to do.

It is the golfer's responsibility to know the rules that apply to caddies, not the caddy's responsibility, because it is the golfer who suffers the penalty if the caddy breaks the rules. On the pro tours the caddy earns a percentage of the prize money won by his golfer, but as amateurs can't win money, it is up to the golfer how they recompense a volunteer caddy. I would suggest a couple of drinks would be the minimum expected.

Apart from one round of golf in Thailand, I have never felt it necessary to employ a caddy.

How about a joke involving a caddy? OK, you've persuaded me.

A rather bad golfer was playing a round on a Scottish course, accompanied by a local caddy. The caddy tried his hardest to offer the golfer advice, but it was always ignored and the golfer's score reflected that.

The golfer played a particularly wayward shot after once again ignoring the caddy's advice to "lay up".

"You must be the worst caddy in the world." The golfer stormed.

"Now, Sirrrrr," the caddy replied. "That would be tooooo much of a coincidence."

Captain

There was a time when the post of captain was always held by the best golfers in the club. This was because the captain was expected to represent the club at other golf clubs (see *Golf Clubs*) and it was a matter of pride that the club's representative should put on a good show when on the course.

When golf clubs were the province of the wealthy and professional classes, the captain had the ability to take time off work to represent their club and also the time and money to develop their game to the level where they became competent enough to hold the post of captain. Being captain was also expensive. At one time the captain was expected to purchase the prizes for certain competitions, such a "Captain's Day". This is still the case in some clubs.

Changes in the game, such as the opening of many more new courses when planning laws were changed for certain types of farmland, made it a lot more egalitarian. It also meant that, at many clubs, members who work for a wage rather than a salary were less able to take time off work to fulfil the duties required of a captain. Clubs adapted to this by concentrating their golfing activities around the weekend, and committee functions around evening meetings, but it still made the pool of potential captains much smaller if being a good golfer was also a requirement.

Consequently, finding a captain these days is more a search for the willing, rather than picking from a short list of those most eligible. It is still considered a great honour to be asked to captain one's club, but you no longer have to play off a sub 10 handicap.

Clubs often have more than one "captain". There will be the "Club Captain", who is the senior representative for that year, but there will also probably be a Lady Captain, a Seniors Captain (see *Seniors*) and a Juniors Captain, each heading up their own section of the club and running competitions for their own groups of golfers.

In addition, there may be different captains appointed to lead teams that compete in inter-club competitions and leagues. Over the summer months the Seniors Section at my club play a series of friendly matches against the seniors of other clubs and we have a small pool of golfers who undertake the role of captain at each match, so as to share the organisational burden.

This system allows me to volunteer my services for the fixtures at the courses that I enjoy playing the most, guaranteeing my inclusion in the team. As a payback, I also captain the corresponding home fixture against the same club.

Having held the post of Senior's Captain at my golf club, I can testify that it isn't all beer and skittles (or G&Ts and golf, if you prefer). Apart from organising competitions, the captain also has to resolve disputes. When these pertain to the rules of golf, the captain can call on the help of the club secretary (see *Secretary*) and the pro, both of whom will know more about the game than anyone else in the club. No, I mean the disputes in the game relating to other issues, such as who had the right to tee-off first when Charlie hadn't arrived to join his group but the next group in line was complete but it wasn't yet their tee-time. I know that the answer sounds simple, but you have probably never had to deal with seniors, who have a lot of time on their hands and are more than willing to spend it splitting hairs.

As for chairing meetings, it is said that work expands to fit the time available in which to do it and seniors have an awful lot of time available.

But being selected to be captain is still an honour.

Cheating and cheats

Most games have an element of cheating in them. Even in the game of rugby, another game I love, it isn't unknown for a player to steal a yard when taking a penalty kick, if the ref isn't looking.

But golf is different.

In golf, being caught cheating is the worst thing that can happen to a golfer. He could be discovered having sex with a goat in the middle of the practice putting green and expect more sympathy than if he was caught cheating.

The reason for this is simple enough: it's all about trust.

Except in the most prestigious competitions, golfers never have a referee accompanying them on the course. They have to "referee" themselves and each other.

Golfers spend a lot of time apart on the course. While one player is on one side of the fairway his partner may be on the other. This distance offers many opportunities for the golfer to play fast and loose with the rules.

But it is when the golfers lose sight of each other that the real opportunities for cheating arise: When the golfer is deep in the woods and there is the possibility of moving a ball from behind a tree to a better position, for example: the possibility of "finding" a ball when in fact it has never been found (see the James Bond film, Goldfinger): the possibility of nudging a ball with the foot to move it from out of bounds (see *Out of bounds*) to legally playable.

Because of these opportunities and many others, golfers have to be able to trust each other, which is why cheating in golf is such a contemptible thing. It isn't just about breaking the rules, it is about having contempt for your friends. Even hardened criminals who would sell their granny at a discount price if it suited them, will balk at cheating at golf.

I knew of one golfer who always played with exactly the same make of ball, always bearing the same number (golf balls, for some reason, are numbered) and always having identical markings made with green ink. This was all a warning that should have been heeded.

While on a golfing "tour" this golfer was in a group further up the field than my group. We had to pass quite close to a green which that group had already reached. One of my partners happened upon a golf ball lying in thick grass behind the green. He examined it and saw the familiar markings used by Ludwig (name chosen for the same reason as I chose Helmut, above). Ludwig, however, was standing several yards away, preparing to take his shot.

"Hey, Ludwig," my partner called. "Your ball's over here."

"No it isn't." Denied Ludwig. "My ball's here." He pointed at his feet.

"Well, this one has your markings on it." my partner said, tossing the ball onto the green where it was examined by the rest of Ludwig's group. I have no doubt a discussion followed, but my group had to move on (see *Slow play*).

On another occasion, actually a corporate golfing event organised by a mutual friend, Ludwig claimed to have found his ball after a lengthy search and played his shot into the green. When the group arrived on the green they found five balls, two of which bore Ludwig's markings. I have never played golf with Ludwig since.

The worst thing about both those stories was that Ludwig was a good golfer and had no need to cheat in order to win against most opposition. He seemed to do it just because he could.

Once someone is suspected of cheating there is nothing for them to do but leave the club. They will be unable to find anyone to partner them for a round of golf and people will shun them in the bar. Everyone will know that they are suspect. If they enter a competition, they will find themselves playing alongside the captain or another committee member, who will follow them around the course like a second shadow. They will never be selected to play for a club team for fear of embarrassing the club in front of the opposition by being caught cheating.

But their problems won't end there. Once they have joined a new club, they will find that their reputation catches up with them. They will be under suspicion when they arrive there and may suffer similar consequences.

With the prizes in golf matches often being as little as a "sleeve"* of golf balls, the risk of being caught cheating far outweighs any benefit that might be gained.

* An oblong cardboard box usually containing three balls.

Chip

To some, this is a golf shot played close to the green with the intention of getting the ball close to the hole, but to most amateurs it is one of a larger number of 'chips' that you order in the clubhouse after the game. Melted cheese on top optional.

Clubs

Unfortunately, there are two meanings for this term, so I have to do twice as much writing to cover them both.

The first type of club is the one you use to hit the golf ball. To find out about the second sort of club, see *Golf Clubs*.

The RoG states that you can have up to fourteen clubs in your golf bag, but no more. Unfortunately, thanks to golf club manufacturers, there are more than fourteen clubs available to choose from. Which clubs the golfer selects is a matter of personal preference, but it is expected that one of them will be a putter.

So, let's go through the different types, so you can make your selection:

Driver: Technically a "1 wood". The heavy artillery of golf, the one you use to get the most distance. Unfortunately, the distance may not be in the direction you want. The greater the distance you hit the ball, the deeper in trouble you may end up. It is also the most expensive club in the bag. At the time of writing the **Maruman Golf's Majesty Prestigio Super7 Driver is thought to be the world's most expensive at** $2,500 (£2,000 approx). Even a run of the mill Ping will set you back about £400.

Woods: They come in a variety of sizes, but the most popular are a 3 and a 5. Used for hitting long shots off the fairway, or more controlled but shorter shots off the tee. Ironically, most woods are now made of metal, but the old name lives on. We amateurs do love our traditions.

Hybrids/rescue clubs: Really just a variation on the 5 wood, they have a "lofted" face and a heavy head which helps to get the ball out of thick rough (see *Rough*) without losing too much distance.

Irons: Numbered 1 to 9. The higher the number, the greater the "loft", i.e. the amount of height the ball gains. Also, the higher the number, the shorter the shaft. For those that remember their high school physics lessons, that means the club head moves slower than for a longer shaft, so less distance is gained. Few amateurs actually use 1 and 2 irons because they are notoriously difficult to get right. There is a joke attributed to Lee Trevino that tells of a golfer dancing around in a thunderstorm waving a 1 iron in the air. Asked why he wasn't worried about getting struck by lightning, the golfer replied "Even God can't hit a 1 iron". Most amateurs prefer to use woods in situations where those low numbered irons might be played.

Wedges: Two basic types, the sand wedge, used for failing to get the ball out of a bunker and the pitching wedge, which plays a high shot into the green so the ball stops dead when it lands (in theory). There are also lob wedges and gap wedges which play similar shots from shorter range. Professionals often carry three or four different wedges in preference to mid-range irons, which they have less of a need for.

Putter: Drive for show, putt for dough, the professionals are alleged to say. The putter can make or break a round. Some amateurs are obsessed with them and some people are forever seeking out "The One". Which means they never achieve any consistency with the ones they have because they never have time to get used to them before they're trying out another new one. Also a very expensive club for those that are willing to pay for perfection. But in reality, you can't buy a putt. It is good technique combined with an ability to "read the green" that makes for good putting. A friend of mine is a demon putter with an ancient brass headed relic he "liberated" from a seaside crazy-golf course many years ago.

Golf club manufacturers are always trying to convince us that their new model of club is the one that will change our golfing lives. Well, they do have product to shift. For the average amateur, new clubs are the least likely thing to make a difference to their game. A lesson with the pro would be far more beneficial and considerably cheaper.

But hope springs eternal, as they say. I never buy the latest offerings, however. I wait until the new models come out, then buy the model that is being replaced as these will be heavily discounted so that the retailer can make room for the new stock. It means I'm always one generation behind the latest technology, but for most amateurs this is like buying last year's model of iPhone.

Golf clubs come with a variety of different types of shaft: Stiff, regular, whippy, graphite, steel, etc. What type of shaft will suit you best can't be explained in a book. The only way to find out is to try them out on the driving range. There is also a certain amount of "fashion" involved. For a while, graphite shafts were all the rage across the board, but now they seem to be confined to woods and drivers, with irons having steel shafts. But if you want graphite shafted irons, they are available. They are lighter and tend to be preferred by children, ladies and older men.

Clubhouse

The clubhouse is the central hub of any golf course. If it is welcoming and comfortable, it encourages the golfer to stay and relax. If it is austere or without atmosphere the golfer would rather go somewhere else.

Unsurprisingly, clubhouses come in all shapes and sizes, from ancient and venerable buildings gifted to the club by the original owner or built when the course was first opened, (You know, when Adam took up the game to get away from Eve's nagging!) through to portacabins that were intended to be replaced but never have been.

Most clubhouses contain the same facilities. Changing rooms and showers for the golfers, a bar, a dining room, and a pro shop. You would think that would make all clubhouses much of a muchness, but it doesn't.

Just like a pub, if it doesn't have any "atmosphere" then it will be shunned. But you can't design atmosphere. That is made by the members. If they are welcoming, chatty and good company, then it is a pleasure to sit after a game and talk about the round, the weather, or whatever the hot topic of the day happens to be - even if the clubhouse is a portacabin.

Sadly, with the prices that clubs have to charge for refreshments, there is little encouragement for members to stay after a round of golf. The norm will be a single drink before they leave. The location of golf courses doesn't help, because they will be outside of built up areas, which means that people have to drive to get there.

But on a sunny day there is nothing nicer than sitting on the terrace (we've got a small one) with a cold beer, watching the other golfers coming down the 18th fairway while you put the world to rights.

Committee

I don't think it would be an exaggeration to say that the committee is the brains behind a golf club. Not all members would agree with that in the intellectual sense, but they are the organ that ensures the rest of the body functions. Even stupid people can breathe, as they say (even if they can't chew gum at the same time).

In clubs owned by the members, the committee will oversee all aspects of the club's functioning, from the state of the drains to deciding if a member has been cheating. There may actually be more than one committee, one for the management of the club and one for the management of golfing activities, but with some commonality of membership between the two.

In clubs that are owned by a third party, the committee mainly oversees the running of competitions and the organisation of social functions, while the club management looks after everything else.

Being on the committee offers considerable influence in the running of the club, so you would think that there would be no problem attracting nominees for election. In practice it is the opposite. Most committees are made up of a handful of the willing and the rest have been pressed into service.

On most committees there are a number of fixed positions:

- Captain - the club's official representative for the year.
- Vice-Captain - the person who does most of the work in organising competitions, in return for which they will be elected Captain unopposed the following year.
- Secretary - the person with the actual power. They liaise with the club management and are the conduit for all correspondence with the county and national golfing authorities. They also write the minutes for all meetings, so the way they remember the discussion is the way it will be recorded.
- Treasurer - looks after the players' money, raised mainly through competition entry fees and advises on how much can be spent on different things. *
- Handicaps Secretary - manages the handicapping system. This is a lot easier now that computers have become involved.
- Seniors and Lady captains, if these sections exist as official entities within the club.

There may also be ad hoc committee members who are expected to represent the views of the members and also to assist the Captain and Vice-Captain. The club manager may also attend committee meetings in an advisory capacity. It cuts out the "middle-man" if he or she is there to hear the discussion.

As we live in a democracy, all the committee members are elected, usually at an Annual General Meeting. But as hinted at earlier, the number of nominees for any post is usually one and sometimes zero, which means that the election is just a formality.

Committees come in for a lot of criticism at times, for either not doing what the members want them to do or for imposing restrictions on what the members may do. With that in mind, I have often suggested that the complainants stand for committee membership in order to make their feelings felt. This usually results in the complainant changing the subject or remembering an urgent appointment elsewhere. But it never stops them complaining again if they can get an audience willing to listen.

Whether you respect the committee or not, without it a golf club would just be a building. Nothing gets organised without someone to organise it and that comes down to the committee. But they get precious little thanks for it.

* Under the RoG, competition entry fees may only be spent on golfing activities and essential administration costs, not on social activities. So, entry fees may be used to buy the prizes for a competition but may not be used to pay for a social evening where the prizes will be handed out. Have your money ready to buy raffle tickets!

Competitions

Not all golfers wish to take part in competitions; some just wish to have a casual round of golf with their pals. At my club, however, competitions are popular and attract big fields. There have even been complaints that some members haven't been able to enter competitions because demand for places was so high. But this isn't the same at all clubs.

Competitions come in many forms. Some are played over more than one round. Our Club Championship competition is played over 36 holes on two consecutive days. The Order of Merit is contested over all twelve monthly medal competitions, with the best eight scores for each competitor counting towards the final placings.

As well as singles competitions, there are also team competitions in pairs, threes or fours, in some of which every score from all the players count, some count only the best one, two, or three scores from the group, and some where players score on some holes but not on others.

There are also different scoring formats, such as stableford (see *Stableford*) and medalford, which is a combination of stroke play and stableford.

Then there are the two big match play competitions (see *Match play*) that most clubs hold, which are the singles knock-out and the doubles knock-out, which are played like the FA Cup, with only the winner of each match going through to the next round.

On top of that are the fun competitions, such as "3 club" which is what it suggests, Texas Scramble, and Pressure Ball (sometimes called Mickey Mouse). The rules for those are sufficiently complicated for me not to wish to spend time here explaining them. If you ever play in those sorts of competitions, someone will explain the rules to you.

Count-back

When professional golfers tie a competition or tournament, they have a play-off to decide who wins. There can only be one Open Champion, after all. But this is also important to them because the difference between first place and runner-up can be several hundreds of thousands of pounds in prize money. For the 2019 Open the difference in prize money was approximately $800,000 (£615,000)*.

But for amateurs, when the final scores are in and it is found that there is a tie, most of the competitors will have gone home, making a play-off impractical unless it's held on another day.

So, in amateur golf there is a system called count-back which is used to sort out tied places; or at least the placings that are contenders to win a prize.

The rules for this are standard across golf, to the best of my knowledge. First off, the score for the second 9 holes played (the back 9 as it is known) is taken and if one player scored better than the other on those holes, that player is deemed to be the winner. If it is still a tie, the scores for the last six holes are taken, then the last 3 holes.

If it is still a tie, the best front 9 is then used, the first 6 holes and then the first 3.

If it is still a tie after that (I have no idea if that has ever happened) then the two golfers fight it out in the car park using swords. No they don't. I suspect if it came to it, the matter would be decided by the toss of a coin.

Many a golfer has been demoted from a prize-winning position to an "also ran" by the use of the count-back system. No one said it was fair, only that it is the accepted way of doing things.

* For lower placings the prize money for each tied place is shared equally between the players. E.g. If there is a 3 way tie for 3rd place, the prize money for 3rd, 4th and 5th places will be added together and shared equally.

Course

The RoG divides a golf course into five areas. The largest is the "general area" which is anywhere within the course boundaries. Course boundaries are defined by the golf club themselves as there are so many variations between clubs.

The other four areas are the teeing ground, the penalty areas, the bunkers and the greens. Each has their own set of rules for what may or may not be done in those areas.

This is no different really, than any other sport, the only real difference being the size of the playing areas. For example, within the penalty area of a football pitch a goalkeeper may handle the ball, but no one else can.

But what of those names that we have got to know and love thanks to thousands of hours of TV commentary? What about the rough, the semi-rough, the heavy rough and so on?

All gone, discarded to the dustbin of history. You won't even find a definition for those in the list of definitions published on the R&A's website. Instead, under winter rules you may find the term "close mown area" (meaning fairway, apron or green) being used to say that you can pick your ball up, clean it and place it within 6 inches of the original spot, but no further forward. This is called "pick and place"). By definition, everywhere else that is not close mown must be something else.

Of course, the golfers themselves still refer to the rough, after all, the average amateur tends to spend more time there than on the fairway (see *Fairway*), but that is a matter of tradition rather than the RoG. Fairway is another word for which there is no definition in the new RoG.

All of that serves to make a golf course sound like a very bland sort of place, but far from it. You will see a greater variety of animals and birds, plants and trees on a golf course than anywhere outside of a zoo or a botanical garden. At one time there were rumours of a giant cat living on or near our course. It was even reported in the local paper. Muntjac deer are seen quite often.

When visiting the Rolls of Monmouth course, I drove through the entrance gate in a slight fog, to see a herd of fallow deer emerge from the mist and cross the road in front of me. It was a beautiful moment. It's also a beautiful golf course.

Each course is unique in its layout and character, some even varying markedly between front and back nines. For example, the course where I play was originally built as a nine hole course, on what had previously been farmland. However the local council, who owned the course at that time, also owned a stretch of land across the road which had once been the park of a large country house (now a very expensive retirement home). They decided to build another eight holes there, to convert the course into eighteen holes*.

The two sides of the course are very different in character especially in relation to the size and positioning of trees. This is quite common on courses which have been upgraded from smaller ones, especially links courses that have managed to acquire property inland from their original course.

I have said elsewhere that each game of golf is unique. This is because the amateur can often find themselves playing from parts of the golf course that they have never visited before. I'm not saying they will find unicorn nests there, but you can encounter features never seen before.

* I know this only adds up to seventeen. The eighteenth hole was built on the same side of the road as the original nine holes.

Course management

I think it is fair to say that if more high handicap amateurs, myself included, paid more attention to course management, their handicaps wouldn't be so high.

In essence, course management isn't really difficult. You just have take a look at each shot before you make it, consider the options and the probability of each option being successful, then choose the option that offers the best probability of success.

Now, what could be easier than that?

First of all you only have two priorities on a golf course:

1. Stay out of trouble, and
2. If you find yourself in trouble, get out of trouble.

That's it! That's course management in a nutshell.

For example, today on our 13th hole my options for my tee shot were to take my driver and probably put my ball in the lake (a much higher probability since they made the lake bigger last year), or take an iron and play a safer shot but not go so far. I went for the iron and the safer shot. It worked and I avoided the lake. That, in course management terms, was the better decision. It wasn't so satisfying in terms of either distance or "style" but as they say, there are no photographs on a scorecard, so style counts for nothing.

In terms of priority two, my decision-making today was far worse. On the 1st hole my ball found its way into some trees (I make it sound like it had nothing to do with me). Given the 100% probability of getting back onto the fairway if I chipped out sideways, or making a shot with a 50% probability (optimistic) of getting back onto the fairway through the trees further along, I made the 50% choice and paid a heavy price. Bad course management.

I don't believe in luck as a concept, so I have to concede that when my shots go wrong and I end up in trouble, it isn't luck that caused them to go wrong, it was my bad choices. But when, on the 17th hole today, I hit a brilliant 3 wood straight along the fairway, only to see the ball hit the ground and bounce sideways into a bunker, I have to wonder if there is someone up there having a laugh at my expense. That shot had nothing to do with course management, good or bad!

Crown

Nothing to do with royal headgear. When the plug of grass and soil is lifted out of the ground to create the hole on the green, it sometimes raises the turf around the hole to leave a slight bulge that deflects the ball away from the hole at the last moment. This is referred to as a 'crown'. It shouldn't happen and the best greenkeepers take great care to prevent it happening, but we've all encountered crowned holes in our time.

Cut, the

Nothing to do with knives or the length of the grass. The cut is what happens to approximately half the competitors in a golf tournament at the halfway stage, usually after 36 holes of play but occasionally after 54 holes, either instead of or as well.

The golfers who will stay for the end of the tournament are said to have "made the cut".

The precise score needed to make the cut varies from tournament to tournament, but the USPGA has a rule for its tournaments. Any player below 70th place doesn't make the cut. If there are tied players in 70th place then all of the tied players may be included, up to a maximum of 78 qualifiers. If there are more than that, the tied players will be excluded to reduce the numbers. To compensate them they will still receive the pay check equivalent to them finishing in 70th place in the competition.

Some tournaments have a "10 shot rule", which means that any player within 10 shots of the leader will make the cut. If this is the case, it will be laid down in the rules for the tournament, but nowadays the 70th place cut-off tends to apply.

D is For

Distance markers

Distance markers are placed on or close to the fairways of golf courses to help the amateur to gauge how far they are from the hole. There is no standard type of distance marker and on an unfamiliar course the amateur may have to work it out for themselves.

I have seen small rocks used as distance markers as well as specific types of tree or bush. More normal are stakes to one side of the fairway, usually green or green and white and sometimes having the distance printed on them, but not necessarily.

Also common are concrete or plastic discs set into the centre line of the fairway itself. These are often plain white in colour, but if more than one disc is in use on the hole they may be colour coded. But there is no standard colour code. On our course they happen to be blue for two hundred yards (only on par 5s), white for one hundred and fifty yards and red for one hundred yards. But I've also seen yellow used for the one-fifty yard marker.

Typically, par 3 holes won't have distance markers because there should be no need for them.

Confused? You will be.

But the really confusing bit is how great the distance is from the marker to the green. Now, given that this is the whole point of them, you would think that would (a) be obvious and (b) be standardised. But it isn't, because some golf clubs measure the distance to the front of the green and some measure to the centre of the green. This can mean a difference of fifteen or twenty yards on a big green. That's between ten and fifteen percent of the total distance. That is a big potential margin of error.

And the club staff don't always know how the measurements have been done because it was "before their time". On more than one occasion I have asked in the pro shop, whose staff should know the answer, only to be told that they didn't have a Scooby*.

Due to changes to the course, some of the distances are also no longer accurate. The use of GPS based distance measuring devices has demonstrated this. Standing next to the one-fifty marker on one hole at a particular course my sat nav told me I was a hundred and ninety yards from the centre of the green, which was the true distance. The hole had been lengthened but the marker disc hadn't been moved. I mentioned this to the club staff when I got back to the clubhouse, to be told "the members always ignore that marker". Not much help to a visitor, though.

The moveable stakes are the worst for being wrong, however. They are taken out when the greenkeepers mow the grass, or when they are in the way of a golfer's stroke and aren't always replaced in the same place. On my own course there can be as much as ten yards difference between the stakes and the discs on the fairway, where the stakes have "crept" forwards or backwards over time.

Place not your trust in distance makers; buy a decent GPS device instead.

Distance markers are of no interest to Pros. They have caddies to walk the course for them and measure everything that is measurable, which measurements are then compiled into "course notes" which the pro can consult so that the pro always knows how far it is from here to anywhere else,. Well, that used to be the way it was done. Nowadays the caddies make the use of technology to do the same thing using satellite imagery.

A conversation allegedly picked up by TV microphones at a golf tournament:

Colin Montgomery "How far is to the hole?"

Caddy "From that sprinkler cover its one hundred and thirty yards precisely."

Colin Montgomery "Yes, but from the back of the drain cover or the front?"

* For non-British readers, this is an example of "rhyming slang". Scooby Doo = clue. To be used with authenticity, only the first word of the rhyme is said. Anyone saying both words is giving themselves away as an imposter.

Divots

A divot is a chunk of grass and/or soil uprooted when a golfer strikes the ball. A golfer should always "take a divot" when they play their stroke - other than on the green, of course. Tiger Woods says he expects his divots to be the size, shape and thickness of a dollar bill. Mine are the size, shape and thickness of a rugby ball.

The important bit about divots is to replace them when you take them. Put the divot back where it came from and press it down firmly with your foot. This helps to maintain the condition of the course, as the grass on the divot will grow new roots and secure it in place. In time it will heal up completely.

Of course, it is easy to say that but many inconsiderate golfers don't do it. This makes it very frustrating when you see your ball nicely in the centre of the fairway but when you get close to it you find that it is lying in the bottom of an old divot hole and it is impossible to get a clean shot on it.

The RoG even anticipates this problem, because the rules say you have to "play the course as you find it", which means divot holes and all.

Amateurs try all sorts of ruses to move their ball from old divot holes, especially trying to claim them as "abnormal ground conditions", but basically, suck it up buttercup. Play the course as you find it - and remember to replace your divots, because the reason you're in that hole is because someone else failed to do so. And it may even have been you!

Actually, there is another reason why divot holes exist. Birds, especially members of the crow family, overturn the divots to try to get at bugs and worms living underneath. So, before you blame your fellow golfers, consider the likelihood of members of the corvus family having committed the offence (the clue is that the divot itself will be right next to the hole rather than several feet away). Then replace the divot yourself for the benefit of other golfers.

The only place you aren't supposed to replace a divot is on the teeing area. This is because a freshly replaced divot makes for insecure footing. Most golf clubs provide a box of loose soil mixed with grass seed that should be used to fill the hole instead. If you see such a filled hole on the teeing area, try to not disturb it when you play your shot.

A divot the size and shape of a rugby ball.

Dog leg

A dog leg is a particular shape of hole on a golf course and implies a bend in the fairway "like a dog's hind leg". They can vary from a slight bend that means the green isn't quite visible from the tee, or a major bend. Our course has one dog leg which has a full ninety degree bend.

    Dog legs are intended to add to the difficulty and length of a golf course, forcing the golfer to take two shots where otherwise they might be able to reach the green in one. To make sure you have to play around the corner rather than over it, some other sort of obstruction, such as trees, are usually in place. Once upon a time our "big hitters" used to shorten the hole by driving over the corner of the dog leg, turning a par 4 into a par 3. The growth of the adjacent trees has put an end to that, but I know of a few of the old hands that are still tempted by it. This is actually quite dangerous because within the angle encompassed by the dog leg are the gardens of a retirement home, so the risk of taking out a resident when cutting the corner is quite high.

But there are rarely any trees on links courses. There you will probably have a blind shot over the sand dunes and if the course designers have done a thorough job, there will be a bunker right in the landing zone ready to gather your ball into its sandy embrace.

If you fail to reach the corner of the dog leg, bringing the green into view, it is quite feasible to turn what should be a simple par into a bogey or even double bogey.

DQ

DQ stands for disqualification. You would think that to earn a DQ would be in the same league as being discovered cheating, but it isn't. DQs are quite common in amateur competitions (they aren't unknown in professional tournaments) and they don't imply cheating.

They do imply a breach of the RoG, however.

There are four basic reasons for a DQ.

(1) Non-compliance with a rule. You would think that would be classed as cheating, but as the rules are complicated and some leeway is granted with regards to knowledge of the rules, a golfer will be DQ'd if it is discovered that they broke a rule without realising they had done it. This will normally include some sort of gathering of evidence by the committee, so the golfer has a chance to justify their actions.

(2) Incorrect application of a penalty. It may be that the player hasn't applied the correct penalty when they took relief or played

another ball. This is granted the same lee-way as non-compliance with a rule, because knowing what penalty to apply under what circumstances is also quite complicated. This would also be subject to some sort of evidence gathering and investigation.

(3) Signing for an incorrect score. This could be an arithmetic error, it could be because a score wasn't recorded correctly or it could be because a penalty wasn't applied.

(4) Failing to sign the scorecard. This is a matter of fact, so doesn't require investigation.

Number (4) is by far the most common reason for being DQ'd. Why this should be is a mystery, as there is a clearly marked space on the scorecard (see *Scorecard*) for the player to sign.

When I was Seniors Captain at my club, hardly a week went by without me having to DQ a member from a competition for failing to sign their scorecard. With seniors this might be expected. After all, they don't call absentmindedness "senior moments" without good reason. But for younger golfers it is harder to find a reason why scorecards aren't signed.

However, some people deliberately don't sign their card, thinking that their score won't count and their handicap won't be adjusted because of it. This might once have been sound reasoning, but most clubs now use a computer to record scores and if the player inputs their score into the computer, it doesn't know if the scorecard has been signed or not, so the card will be used to make adjustments to handicaps.

DQ is a manual adjustment of the score on the computer that is carried out after the event. The golfer is then treated in the same way as a "nil return" (not submitting any scorecard at all because the score was so bad or the player had to abandon their round) and the golfer's handicap will be increased by point one of a stroke. Under the forthcoming changes to the World Handicapping System (WHS), clubs will be able to input "penalty scores" for unsigned cards to prevent this sort of handicap protection.

If a player is being consistently DQ'd for the same or similar reasons, they will be taken outside and beaten with a 9 iron.

No, they won't. Just joking. The Captain or Secretary will take them to one side and have a chat with them, explaining the rules in words of one syllable and that will be the end of the matter. Only if the golfer continues to transgress will more serious action be considered.

So, being DQ'd isn't the same as cheating, it is just a sign that the golfer doesn't understand the rules as well as he should, or that he is suffering from a poor memory.

Dress code

This is something of a regular topic of discussion amongst amateurs, especially those in clubs that have less of a history.

Back in the days when golf clubs were owned and run by the wealthy and professional classes, rigid dress codes were enforced. It was a way of keeping the riff-raff out as much as anything else. But it was also a reflection of society as a whole. At a time when people still dressed in "black tie" to go out for dinner, they expected similar standards to be maintained in their clubs (not just golf clubs).

But times have changed. Not only does society as a whole dress differently these days, there is also competition for membership. Any club that relies on the wealthy and professional classes to keep it alive is likely to go bust quite quickly so the vast majority of clubs have had to become much more egalitarian. With that egalitarianism comes a much wider range of views about what is appropriate in terms of dress. There are still the traditional bastions of the golfing world, but they are now the exception, not the rule.

With the exception of municipal courses (I'll return to them later), most golf clubs still enforce some sort of dress code for when golfers are actually on the course. Some people may rail against that, but I look at it this way: If you play football you will wear a recognisable type of kit: football boots, knee length socks, football shorts, football shirt. The same applies to rugby, cricket, basketball, tennis etc. Each has its own "dress code". So why should golf be any different?

The dress code for wear on the course that is requested by golf clubs isn't demanding. Golf shoes, trousers (not jeans), or "tailored" shorts usually with knee length socks. Shirts generally have to have a collar and sleeves (long or short). Shirts more appropriate to other sports (such as replica footballs shirts) aren't allowed, neither are shirts with non-golfing logos or slogans. I really don't think that is asking too much of the golfer.

Off the course the discussion gets more heated. When dress codes are imposed for wear in the bar, people aren't so keen. In some clubs the clothes worn on the golf course aren't allowed to be worn off it. In some clubs jeans are allowed, in other they aren't. In some clubs jeans are allowed in the casual bar (if there is one) but not in the members' lounge. And so on and so forth.

I recall playing in a corporate event (a friend and I were making up the numbers). It was held at an old, well established club in Shropshire. After playing nine holes in the morning we were to have lunch before going out to play eighteen holes in the afternoon. On arrival at the clubhouse for lunch, my friend was informed that he couldn't wear his shorts in the dining room; he had to wear long trousers. Having none, he hastily borrowed a pair of mud caked waterproof trousers. These, it seemed, were OK.

Mud caked trousers, because they were long, were acceptable but not a pair of clean and perfectly respectable looking shorts. Go figure.

But rules is rules!

When I first started playing for the seniors team at our friendly fixtures with other clubs, we always ate our after match meal wearing a jacket and tie (and trousers and shirts too - thought I'd better clarify). Some clubs we play still request that. Other clubs, like my own, have relaxed that down to "smart casual" and even "golfing attire", depending on the style of meal that is to be eaten. For some fixtures the meal will be chips and sandwiches and people don't really want to have to dress up for that, while at others it will be a carvery meal and a bit of dressing up is more appropriate.

Municipal courses are those that are owned by the local council. Some will be operated as a franchise, while others will be directly managed. It doesn't matter which management type they have, the purpose of the municipal course is to allow anyone who wants to play golf to be able to do so. If dress codes are imposed, on or off the course, that participation is discouraged.

On one municipal course I was visiting, near Coventry, I saw a group of lads playing in beach shorts and singlets, one of whom was wearing flipflops, the rest trainers. It was a hot day and they were dressed for the heat rather than for the game. Their behaviour on the course matched their attire, with a lot of shouting and yelling going on and very little attention was being paid to any damage that the course might suffer as a result of their play (see *Divots* and *Pitch marks*).

That sounds judgemental, I know, but it discouraged me from playing that course again, even though the course itself is a good challenge. I'm not saying that white tie and tails would have improved their behaviour (Bullingdon Club anyone?) but the act of getting changed into golfing attire might have made the lads stop and think about where they were and honouring the game, rather than just playing it.

Rant over. I suspect the debates over dress code will continue long into the future. My advice to the amateur who is visiting another club for the first time, is to check out the club's dress code before the visit, so as not to end up in an argument with the club management or committee - or having to wear mud caked waterproof trousers in the dining room.

By the way, brightly patterned trousers, tartan trousers (known as Rupert Bears) etc are only worn as a joke, despite what many non-golfers think. If you wear them because you think that is what golfers normally wear, you have fallen victim to a joke.

On the golf course, professional golfers wear the clothes they are sponsored to wear, or they are promoting their own brand of golf clothing. This branded clothing is always twice as expensive as the perfectly acceptable alternatives that are available in any high street store.

Drive

Also known as a tee-shot, the drive is the shot that amateurs take the most pride in. It is unsurprising. There is no more beautiful sight in golf than to see one's ball arc skywards on the perfect line to find the centre of the fairway some two hundred plus yards away.

It's a pity that the average amateur sees it so rarely.

The shot is called a "drive" because it is played with a "driver", previously known as a 1 wood (see *Clubs* and *Woods*). The name has changed since the introduction of drivers with oversized heads which bear no resemblance to a 1 wood. It also means that the manufacturers are able to sell the driver as a separate item at an exorbitant price, rather than as a set of three matching woods at a cheaper price.

Golfers have been known to spend hours on the driving range or practice ground (see *Driving range*) practicing their drives, which is a pity. Their time would be more profitably spent on the putting green practicing their putting.

Think about it. The average golf course has thirteen or fourteen holes where a driver may be the club of choice to use on the tee. But it has eighteen greens. Taking three putts on a green is far worse in terms of returning a good score than miss-cuing a drive so that it only goes a hundred yards.

While I enjoy the sight of a good drive as much as anyone, I am far more satisfied by sinking a twenty foot putt. That doesn't mean I spend a lot of time practicing my putts, it just means I get more enjoyment out of the rare occasions I make a twenty foot putt.

Driving range

The driving range is an area set aside for the golfer to practice their shots. The term implies a covered area with a bay for each golfer, a mat from which they can play their shots and some sort of markers for them to aim at. On some golf courses the area isn't so well served and is more probably going to be called the "practice ground", but it has the same purpose. At some golf clubs the practice area may be no more than a net strung up on a frame, into which the golfer can hit shots without risk of hitting other golfers.

One thing you will often see on TV coverage of golf, especially early in the day when the course is still quite empty of competitors to watch, is scenes of the pros out on the driving range practicing for their game. This is more than just them practicing their shots, however. It is also warming up their muscles ready for the start of the game. All athletes warm up in advance, with good reason; it helps to prevent muscular injuries.

It is quite common amongst amateurs for them to complain of muscular pains while playing and the lack of a proper warmup might be a contributing factor. I'm not a sports scientist, so that is just an observation.

It is generally true that amateurs don't spend nearly enough time on the driving range, either as a warmup or for genuine practice. The higher the handicap, the truer this is. While the driving range can't replicate the conditions that will be found on the course, it does help the golfer to identify if things are going wrong. If you can't hit a ball properly on a driving range, you don't stand a chance of hitting it properly on the golf course.

The driving range allows the golfer time to analyse what they are doing, identify poor technique and try to put it right. That time simply isn't available during a round of golf.

But for the amateur to use the driving range before a round of golf it means them having to arrive at the course half an hour or more earlier and few amateurs are willing to sacrifice that time. Which is a pity, because it is usually time well spent.

I always spend time on the driving range, warming up and practicing my shots. No, I'm lying. I'm as bad as every other amateur when it comes to practice.

With driving ranges come practice balls, aka "range balls". While these often bear the logo of well-known manufacturers, they are also marked as range balls because (a) the club doesn't want golfers stealing them and (b) they aren't actually of the same quality as normal balls.

A range ball is specifically manufactured for use on the driving range. Accordingly, it is more hard wearing because it is unlikely to be replaced at regular intervals and it is going to be hit by golfers of widely varying ability. This difference in manufacture has a significant effect on the distance that a range ball will travel. Typically the distances are only 80% of what can be achieved with a regular golf ball, even a poor quality one. Distances are also variable depending on whether the ball is hit from grass or a mat and whether it is wet or dry.

But distance isn't what matters on the driving range. It is technique that is being assessed because it is technique that the amateur is trying to improve: Did the ball fly straight, or did it slice or hook? If it sliced or hooked, why did it do that? A good shot will still be apparent, even if it only flies seventy or eighty percent of the distance. It just won't feel so satisfying!

The pros don't use range balls for their pre-game practice. They are all provided with the identical golf balls, which have been stamped "practice". In all respects they perform as well as the balls that the pro will be use on the course itself. Most of these balls are supplied by the Titelist brand, but other manufacturers can bid for the contract. The ball is only ever hit once, before being retrieved and repackaged for sale as second hand.

E is For

Eagle

Unsurprisingly, an eagle is a much rarer bird than a birdie, at least for the amateur. Your author has had two eagles in his golfing career, one on a par 4 that was being played from the lady's tee (fifty yards further forward than the men's tee) and one on a par 5 when, for reasons not fully understood, his second shot just kept on rolling all the way to the edge of the green and he then got lucky with his chip (see *Chip*) onto the green. The former was witnessed by almost an entire golfing society (see *Societies*) who were waiting on a tee that overlooked the green, thus earning himself an unaccustomed and probably undeserving round of applause.

The origins of the term are once again The Country Club in Atlantic City where A B Smith claims that players in his group referred to a double birdie as an eagle, in deference to his original use of the word Birdie. This is unverified.

What is known is that in 1919 the word first appeared in Britain when Mr H D Gaunt stated that when he had played golf in the USA and Canada, his North American partners had used both the terms birdie and eagle. PG Wodehouse certainly used the term in writing in 1926 in his novel "The Heart of a Goof".

An unexpected eagle.

Encouragement (words of)

While there are some who believe that banter is all about insulting your playing partners, generally speaking golfers are quite nice to each other on the golf course and are always willing to offer words of encouragement when things don't work out well. So here's a selction of things that are often said and the circumstances wjich cause them to be said.

- Having Just hit your ball into the trees or out of bounds: It was a good strike, the wind got hold of it a bit though.
- Having just landed in water: Well, at least you know where it is.
- Having just topped the ball and sent it only a few yards: At least it went straight.
- Having topped a ball and sent it bouncing along the fairway: That's a worker; look, it's still going.
- Having just taken three shots to escape a bunker: Well, you got out eventually.
- Having missed a putt from two feet away from the hole: I think that hole may be crowned,
- Having missed the hole by a wide margin to one side: Good weight, the line was tricky to read.

There are others, but I'm sure you get the idea.

Equipment

If you think that a golfer's equipment is made up of golf clubs and golf balls and that's all, you are mistaken.

Golfers have no end of equipment that has nothing much to do with actually hitting a ball.

First of all are the golf shoes. The vast majority of golf clubs insist that proper golf shoes are worn on the golf course. This is because golf shoes have spikes, which help to stop golfers sliding around and falling over, especially in wet conditions. Golf shoes come in various brands and styles and have different types of sole and gripping systems. If you want to wear them for more than a year, don't go cheap and cheerful. When it comes to shoes it's definitely a case of buy cheap, buy twice. There is nothing worse in the middle of winter than feeling icy cold water seeping into your socks because of splits in your shoes.

Next there is the golf bag. This is essential for the carrying of golf clubs (and all sorts of smaller items of equipment). Have you ever tried to carry fourteen lengths of steel (or titanium if you are rich) tube around with you? It's like trying to wrestle an octopus. So you need a golf bag.

Younger golfers tend to carry their golf bag over their shoulder or on their back, taking it off to make each shot. Carrying on the back is considered more ergonomically sound than carrying over one shoulder. But as you get older and the body becomes less resilient, most golfers start to use the next essential item of equipment, which is a golf trolley. These come in many shapes and sizes and the cost varies accordingly. A simple two wheeled "pull along" trolley can be bought for as little as £30 ($35), but no one is using them anymore.

Sports scientists (or maybe canny manufacturers) have decided that dragging a trolley around is bad for the back, so modern trolleys have three wheels and are pushed. That extra wheel costs in the range of £70 ($80) as the price of a three wheeler is from £100 upwards.

Then we go to battery powered trolleys, as they require far less effort to guide around the course. These start from about £200 but can go much, much higher. Some are even remote controlled, which is a bit scary when you see one speeding across the fairway towards you, apparently out of control.

One quick story about a powered trolley and its owner. I was playing golf at a local club (not my own) when one of my partners turned his powered trolley on and just let it roll along in front of him without him holding onto the handle. The fairway went downhill, getting quite steep in parts. Unsurprisingly the trolley speeded up, forcing my partner to run after it. He was far too slow, however, and the trolley ended up tipping itself into a lake at the bottom of the hill. He got very wet trying to retrieve it.

But that isn't the end of the story. When we eventually got back to the clubhouse, he discovered that his car keys, which had been in one of the pockets of his golf bag, were no longer there. He had to borrow a buggy and go out to the hole where his bag had met its watery doom and slosh around in the mud until he found his keys. He did find them, though.

But the story doesn't quite end there. Many years later I was reading an interview with a pro in a golf magazine (I was at the doctor's surgery, about the only place where I ever read golf magazines). One of the questions the pro was asked was "What was the funniest thing you've ever seen on a golf course?" The answer was the story I recount above (only he didn't know about the lost car keys). It's a small world!

So, if you want to kit yourself out with a pair of shoes (£80 plus), a set of clubs (£500 plus), a golf bag (£60 to £100) and a powered trolley (£200 minimum) you are looking at the thick end of a grand to get started in the game

I would suggest a visit to a well-known auction website site and look for a second-hand set of clubs, a cheap bag and a reconditioned trolley. If you like the game, you can always upgrade later.

But that will only get you started. If you want to play in the British summer you will need waterproof clothing (£100 plus depending on brand). Golf balls are constantly getting lost and have to be replaced (see a story I tell later under the heading of "water"). Here's a tip; always put golf balls on your Christmas list and specify the brand you prefer. They will never go to waste. Even if you end up with a dozen boxes of the things, they will always come in handy for raffle prizes down at the golf club.

Those are the "big ticket" items, but you will also regularly spend money on towels (mainly for winter use), tee pegs, pitch mark repairers and ball markers.

And if you have read the topics of accessories and aids and are taken in by the clever marketing, you can expect to spend even more money over time.

Author's note: All prices quoted were found on the internet in January 2020.

Etiquette

To some people this word may mean holding one's pinkie out when drinking a cup of tea (I don't think anyone has ever really done that), but in golf it just means having consideration for other golfers. You don't have to have been born with a silver spoon in your mouth to display good manners on a golf course.

The RoG used to have a whole section on etiquette, but this has now been replaced with "Standards of Player Conduct". It is basically the same thing. The emphasis these days is on keeping the game moving, so the old ways of giving the "honour" of teeing off to the player with the lowest score, and playing the ball furthest from the hole before playing those closer to it, have all gone by the board.

Nowadays we are encouraged to play "ready golf" (see *Ready golf*).

It has always been considerate for golfers to stand still and remain silent when their partner is playing their shot, but that consideration goes further. Golf courses aren't the place for shouting your head off. Your partners may not be making a shot, but there may be other golfers nearby who are. They, too, deserve your consideration.

But the basics are simple, golfers should always be considerate towards other golfers: replace divots, rake bunkers, repair pitch marks, be ready to play your shot and keep up with the group in front. That last one is always worth remembering. You should always be one stroke behind the group in front, not one stroke in front of the group behind.

F is For

Fairway

The fairway used to be mentioned a lot in the RoG but now it doesn't even have its own definition. Now it is just part of the "general area".

I remember as a young man reading a humorous book by a sports journalist named Michael Green*, called "The Art Of Course Golf". He wrote a series of books on a wide range of course sports and pastimes (football, rugby, cricket, sailing and more). The "course" is used to differentiate the game from that played by the professionals and other skilled practitioners. In this case Green described "course golf" as a game where the players hit a ball from tee to green without touching the fairway. He also said you could identify course golfers from a distance, because when they left the tee they all went in different directions.

I didn't really understand how that could happen until I came to take up the game myself.

The fairway is the strip of short cut grass along which the golfers are supposed to play, rather than the thicker grass, shrubbery, trees, bunkers and water where we often play the game. The grass is cut short to make it easier for us to (a) find the ball and (b) make our next shot. It is our own fault if we don't avail ourselves of this sacred ground.

Of course, being on the fairway doesn't guarantee the quality of the next shot. You can be in the wrong position on the fairway and find your route to the green interfered with by overhanging trees and there will probably also be bunkers and/or water between you and the green, but at least on the fairway you have a fighting chance of getting to where you want to be. Off the fairway things get a lot more difficult.

* Sadly, Michael Green's books don't appear to be available as e-books and I think the only places you'll find paper copies now are second-hand bookshops or libraries (if you can find one of those these days as well). But if you can find them, do read them if you enjoy the humorous side of sport.

Ferret

Slang name for a chip shot from the side of the green that ends up in the hole, like a ferret chasing a rat. A "sandy ferret" is the same result achieved from a bunker. It is one of the many ways a high handicap (see *Handicap*) amateur can make a birdie or even an eagle

Flag and flag stick

The flag and the stick on which it is mounted indicates the position of the hole so you can see where it is from a distance and aim your shot accordingly. The flag stick used to be thing of great reverence which the ball was never allowed to touch, so it had to be removed from the hole before the ball reached it.

There were many myths about the flag stick and one of the most enduring and inaccurate was that you couldn't have the flag stick "tended" if you weren't on the green. In other words, your caddy or partner couldn't stand next to the flag stick, ready to remove it when your ball got close to the hole.

While that may once have been the case, the rule changed long before I started to play the game, but for some people the rule change had passed them by and they didn't know that and I upset more than a few when I told them they were wrong. I actually went to the trouble of checking with the pro at my golf club and he showed me the relevant rule in the book. You could have the flag stick tended if you were still on the tee if you wanted it, though persuading someone to go and tend it for you would be somewhat of a challenge.

Having said that, it is now a moot point anyway.

In 2019 that rule changed and you can now putt with the flag in whenever you feel like it without fear of incurring a penalty. The majority of golfers seem to be doing that, even for very short putts.

One of the questions that is heard most often on a golf course is "how far is it to the flag?" (sometimes referred to as "the pin") The answer to which is supposed to help the golfer judge their shot. One of the golfing aids that can be purchased is an optical device to measure this distance with a reasonable degree of accuracy.

Distance markers (see *Distance markers*) may tell you how far it is to the front or the centre of the green, but if the flag isn't situated in the relevant place there can still be a considerable margin for error, because greens can sometimes be quite large. So, some golf clubs help the golfer by indicating where the flag is on the green. Some put a collar or a smaller flag on the flag stick which is moved up and down, depending on where the hole is. If the collar is at the top of the stick the hole is at the back of the green and if it is near the bottom the hole is towards the front.

At my club we use different coloured flags to indicate the hole's position: red front, yellow middle and blue rear. You have no idea how hard it is to see a red or a blue flag against a dark background, such as pine trees.

I know some golf course that issues a little card showing plans of all eighteen greens, divided into quarters and labelled A to D or even into sixths labelled A to F. Before you tee off on the first hole you will be told that "Today all the holes are in section … (whatever).

All of the above assistance, however, is dependent on the greenkeepers (see *Greenkeepers*) actually changing the position of the collar, the colour of the flag or using the correct portion of the green, when they cut a new hole. I have played on greens where the pin was at the front but had a yellow flag, which rather defeats the purpose of having a system in the first place.

Flag poles.

There are two reasons for a golf club to have a flag pole.

The first is so that a flag can be flown whenever the Club Captain buys a round of drinks.

The second reason is to fly a flag at half mast when a member dies.

The latter occasion is seen far more often than the former.

Flatulence

As with many sports, the body's digestive system often interferes with the playing of golf. More than once, a golfer's back swing has been interrupted by a less than musical accompaniment from playing partners. If golfers are suffering from digestive trouble, it is considered polite to move away from any players who are taking their stance in preparation for a shot. About a hundred yards is considered adequate.

After revealing the cover for this book on Facebook, I was contacted by a friend in Ireland who told me of a lady friend of hers who was getting golf lessons from an elderly club member. Unfortunately, every time he set himself up to demonstrate a shot for her, he broke wind repeatedly. After the event she re-enacted the whole lesson to her friends in the pub, complete with sound effects, which caused some amusement.

Happy ending, she was able to copy his golfing style without the accompanying soundtrack.

Fore!

Fore is the word of warning shouted by golfers when they think their ball is in danger of striking someone. But why this word?

Its use was first recorded in 1857 in a glossary of golfing terms (presumably much like this one, only not so good) and it appeared in the Oxford English Dictionary for the first time in 1878.

The most likely explanation for the origin of the term is back in the bad old days when golf balls were made of hand carved beech wood and far more expensive in real terms than they are now. For this reason golfers employed "forecaddies", paying them a few pence to stand along the side of the fairway to keep an eye out for where the ball went so as not to lose it. It is possible that "fore" is a shortened version of this, shouted to warn the forecaddie that the ball had just been struck and was on its way towards them. The record of forecaddies being employed goes back to at least 1681 at the Edinburgh Golf Links.

There is another story which has an outside chance of being the correct origin of the shout. It relates to the fire and brimstone Scottish preacher John Knox (1505(ish) - 1570). He relates a story of the firing of two great artillery pieces at the East Port (east gate) of Edinburgh Castle and the gunner shouting "Ware Before" to friendly soldiers near the gate, warning them that the guns were about to be fired towards them. From this it is assumed that the "ware" part was dropped and the "before" part became shortened.

Whatever the true origin was, it is an unusual round of golf where you don't hear someone shouting "Fore" at the top of their voice at some point.

If you hear it, do try to put something solid between you and the person who did the shouting. Even ducking behind your trolley is better than nothing.

Fore!

Four ball

The most common size of group for playing a round of golf, especially social (non-competitive) golf.

Many golf clubs that have a high demand for visitors to play, such as St Andrews, will only allow four-balls out on the course. If you haven't got four in your group, they will allocate single visitors to join you and if you are a single visitor you will be assigned to make up the numbers in a four-ball.

Four-balls are also a common group size for team competitions held by golf clubs. The team with the best score being the winners of the competition.

Two of my appearances on one of the "honours boards" at my club are thanks to my making up the numbers in groups that were a man short. I hasten to add that I did make a contribution to the teams' combined scores, so my places on the board are deserved.

Front 9 and Back 9

By tradition, the eighteen holes of a golf course are divided into two lots of nine. The first nine played is known as the "front 9" and the second nine played is the "back 9".

The layout and numbering of the scorecards used at my golf course is such that the course can be played front nine first or back nine first, depending on what the club decides on a particular day. This is particularly significant for 9 hole competitions, as one lot of nine holes is much longer than the other.

On many golf courses the front nine and back nine are differentiated by having flags of differing colours marking the holes on the greens. Typically these will be red for one nine and yellow for the other. This can be important for visitors. If you find yourself playing towards a flag that is a different colour to the one you expected, it could mean you're playing the wrong hole.

This is no longer the case on my course because we have a three-colour code for the flags which indicates to the golfer whether the hole is at the front, middle or rear of the green (providing the greenkeeper hasn't forgotten to change the flag).

G is For

Gambling

If there is any form of competition in a sport, there will be those who will gamble on the outcome. Let's face it, there are those who will gamble on two raindrops running down a windowpane. Those with a fondness for gambling (I am not one of them) will always want a bet and they will often bet on their own performance.

As with so much else in the game of golf, gambling is covered by the RoG, in this case an appendix to the rules governing amateur status.

Essentially gambling should only be for stakes that aren't considered "excessive". No definition is provided for "excessive", so what I might regard as excessive and what Donald Trump may regard as excessive will be two different things. The second stipulation about gambling is that only those golfers actually involved in a game may gamble on its outcome, so someone watching from the clubhouse terrace shouldn't be making a wager on whether or not a golfer will make a putt.

This is a rule that is ignored by all the gambling companies in the world. You can make a wide variety of bets on the outcomes of tournaments and, thanks to "in play betting", on whether a player golfer will make a putt. But the R&A can't impose its rules on them, so the betting companies don't have to observe them

The final word on gambling is that it should be done for enjoyment, not for financial gain. I see this as contradictory, as what's the point of gambling if not for financial gain? Regardless of the size of the wager, one or more golfers will be financially better or worse off as a direct consequence of the bet. As for enjoyment, I have never enjoyed handing over my hard-earned money.

Gimme

To concede a short putt that would be more difficult to miss than to make, usually from less than 18 inches (45 cm).

The word is an abbreviation of "Give me" as in "will you give me that putt?" which makes it totally incorrect in its usage as it isn't normal to ask for a "gimme"; it is a favour that is granted without being requested.

Gimmes may only be granted in social golf (see Social golf) or in match play (see Match play) as in most competitions the ball must go into the hole before the score can be counted.

I once overheard the following conversation:

Golfer A (bending over to pick up his ball) "That's a gimme then."

Golfer B "What do you mean, 'a gimme? You're at least three feet from the hole."

Golfer A "But we agreed that anything under four feet was a gimme."

Golfer B "No we didn't. What I said was that anything under four feet was a pygmy."

Boom tish!

Greens

The greens are the most sacred ground of golf. Courses can get away with a lot in terms of their quality and presentation, but if their greens are poor, they will lose members and discourage visitors.

Golf clubs receive more complaints about the condition of their greens than they do about the quality of their food.

In terms of the RoG the green is actually referred to as the putting green and is defined as follows:

"The area on the hole the player is playing that:

- Is specially prepared for putting, or

- The Committee has defined as the *putting green* (such as when a temporary green is used)."

To me that definition isn't very helpful, so how do you know that you are on a putting green? Well, first of all it will have a hole cut into it somewhere, which that definition doesn't even mention. Secondly that hole will have a stick emerging from it and on the end of that stick there should be a flag.

Although care of the greens is primarily a task for the greenkeepers (see *Greenkeepers*), it is something that all golfers should consider. If you take care of your greens, your greens will take care of you. I will cover this again under "Pitch marks", but generally, if you damage the greens in any way, you should repair the damage before leaving the green.

You may only repair the damage caused by others after you have completed the hole, except for pitch marks and spike marks. This because you must "play the course as you find it" and damage done by other golfers falls into that category. However, fixing the damage after you have finished putting is a good deed and will be rewarded in Heaven.

If you don't repair the damage, then expect karma to strike at some point. At some time in the future you may have to putt over the damaged area that you didn't repair. Karma can be a bugger sometimes.

Several times a year the greens are subjected to maintenance to keep them in condition. This comes in two forms. The first is "hollow tining" which lifts plugs of grass and earth out of the green to aerate it. The other form is "scarifying" (something gardeners sometimes do to their lawns) to remove dead grass and other detritus from the surface. Both turn putting into a bit of a lottery, but this maintenance is essential if you want to putt on good greens for the rest of the year. The damage normally only takes a couple of weeks to heal naturally, so bear with it. Besides, the damage will affect all golfers equally. The result should be a better surface on which to putt.

When I was one of the organisers for our village golf society, I used to listen very carefully to what our members said about the condition of the greens on the courses we played. Several never saw us again because the members didn't like the condition of their greens. Given that we were paying between £400 to £500 to play there, voting with our feet was the only way we could get the message across to some golf clubs.

Goodness knows how they ever managed to keep members.

Green fee

This the charge made for playing a golf course. It is always expressed in the singular, for some reason, although the course may have more than one fee that they charge depending on time of day, season etc. It is different from a membership fee, though some people interchange the term.

The term "green fee" first appears around 1905, so I assume that it was around then that visitors started to play as anything other than guests of a club member and were therefore charged a fee for their visit. Why the term "green" was attached rather than entrance, visitor, or some other word is something I haven't been able to discover.

If you are just taking up golf and don't want to commit to the expense of joining a golf club (which might be quite considerable) and there is no local society that you can join, then the alternative is to pay a green fee whenever you want to play at your local golf course. When visiting a golf club, you will always have to pay a green fee, unless you are playing in a competition. For competitions any green fee is usually included in the competition entry fee.

Failing to pay the relevant green fee will result in being ejected from the course, as it is the equivalent of theft.

A green fee can vary considerably and are also seasonal. In the middle of winter you might be able to play 18 holes for as little as £15 on a weekday, but in high summer at the weekend the same golf course might charge you £40 or more. Some courses also offer 9 hole rounds, which are cheaper. £15 may sound expensive, but you would pay £12 or more to go to the cinema to watch a two hour film.

There are websites where you can go to book a tee-time at preferential rates, so they are worth checking out, but these usually require you to be a four-ball. If it is just you and a pal you may still have to book direct with the golf club. The club may also do special offers, such as a four-ball "sunset" round, which would mean teeing off at 3 pm or later, but are a real bargain at some of the more expensive clubs. Obviously, those sorts of offers are also seasonal.

If you know someone who is a member of a golf club, see if they'll be willing to invite you along as a guest. You'll still have to pay a green fee, but members' guests are usually offered a discount. If you like the course, see if they will offer you a part year membership so that you can play there regularly. There are often discounts for winter memberships or for the last 3 or 4 months of the year, before annual memberships come up for renewal.

Ultimately there is the green fee for of a round of golf at one of the prestigious golf clubs. These can vary from £100 per person upwards (see *St Andrews*), but it is something you can put on your Christmas list. I've played Celtic Manor, near Newport in Wales, twice thanks to considerate relatives.

Greenskeepers

These men and women are the unsung heroes of golf. It is them we have to thank for the smoothness of our greens, the shortness and picturesque striping of the fairways, the soft, well raked sand in our bunkers and, in autumn, the lack of leaves on our golf courses. They empty the litter bins, they cut up and take away the fallen trees and branches and generally keep things looking nice.

Having said that, they can be a right pain in the backside.

Greenkeepers get their name from the days when the green was the only part of the golf course that was maintained. Sheep were generally used to keep the grass on the fairways short, but the greenkeepers used handheld clippers to get the grass shorter, but still nothing like the miniscule length that can be achieved using modern mowers.

It seems that on some days, the green keepers are always in the way when we want to take our next shot. This is particularly the case when it comes to mowing the greens. If you encounter them on the first green it is almost inevitable that they will be on every subsequent green for the rest of your round of golf.

I have always wondered why they don't start on the 18th green and work their way back towards the 1st. That way, each group as they pass through whatever green they meet the green keepers on, will only have to wait for that one hole, then they will be past them.

But no, they always start on the 1st and keep pace with you all the way round.

Greenkeepers are most evident on weekday mornings. They start work when the sun rises and are usually finished by lunchtime in the summer, somewhat later in the winter. So if you only play your golf at the weekend you wouldn't really know they existed, except for the condition of the course. It doesn't get that way by the use of fairy dust and three wishes!

But for midweek golfers they can be something of a nuisance.

But if you do see a greenkeeper, please do tell them what a great job they are doing. Hardly anyone ever does, but without them the game would be a lot less enjoyable and a lot more difficult.

Gross and nett

Simply put, gross is the number of strokes you actually take when you go around the golf course. Nett is the score you end up with after you have deducted your handicap allowance. I'll be covering this in more detail under both "handicap" and "scoring".

Golf Club

To an outsider one golf club appears to be much like another. Nothing could be less true. The difference between the club where I play and, for example, Royal St George's, is the difference between sailing First Class on the Titanic and sailing "steerage". And, ultimately, it makes about the same difference when it comes to our fate. If the ship is going to sink, all that really matters is that you get a seat in the lifeboat. When we get to the Pearly Gates, however, the member of Royal St George's will have to book his tee-time just like me and we may end up in the same four-ball. That will come more as a shock to him than to me.

The oldest golf club in the world is St Andrews, which dates from 1754. There are two older organisations that played golf, The Royal Burgess Golfing Society and the Honourable Company of Edinburgh Golfers, but they either didn't own their club or their original course no longer exists.

Top of the pecking order are the "members' clubs" that, like St Andrews, have a history going back centuries. Most of them were founded by people with money and status for the express purpose of playing golf with other people who had money and status.

Such clubs do their best to keep out people they don't want. Sometimes this is achieved by having strict membership rules. It wasn't until July 2019 that Muirfield allowed the first women to become members and that was only because they risked losing their place on the rota to host The Open if they didn't admit females. Another way to keep the membership "exclusive" is to make it too expensive for most people to join. Finally, those clubs often require the committee to approve all applications for membership, which means it isn't difficult to block applications from "the wrong sort of people".

The whole point of golf as a social game is that you play with your pals and these are the people who live in the same streets, drink in the same pubs and work in the same sorts of jobs as we do. For us there are plenty of clubs that are more than willing to take our membership fees, no questions (or very few questions) asked.

These are generally clubs that have a single owner, or a small partnership and which either leases the course to the club members or operates the club on their behalf, leaving it up to the golfers themselves to organise the competitions and social activities. The membership fees for the club just make up another line in the owner's profit and loss accounts, while the members get the benefits of having a course to play on, a club house, changing rooms, showers, a bar, dining room etc.

For most of these clubs there are no joining fees and the membership fees are competitive with other clubs in the local area. They have to be, because competition for members has forced the closure of many golf clubs over recent years. The financial crisis of 2007 didn't just hit the banks, it also hit a lot of businesses, which meant they could no longer afford to fund golfing days for their sales teams and customers, which were a nice little earner for golf clubs. When people lose their jobs, the first thing they economise on is their leisure activities, so golf club memberships were heavily impacted.

Attracting new business, whether it be societies, casual golfers or new members is a major marketing task for most clubs these days and the line between survival and going under is a very thin one. *

Needless to say, the quality of the course and the club is heavily dependent on the qualities of the ownership and management team. At my club this is good and I enjoy being a member there. I can't imagine moving. But at another club, not too distant, the last two owners did a runner leaving mountains of debt and the present owner is something of a Richard Cranium and the members are drifting away as their memberships come up for renewal. Several are going to come to our club, so we will benefit. I think it can only be a matter of time before the other club goes to the wall again.

Next in line are the clubs that are attached to hotel chains. While the venues themselves are nice and the courses are usually well cared for, actually being a member at one of these courses isn't always a good experience. I was a member at a local hotel course for three years and I always felt like a second-class citizen. The hotel management didn't have any time for the members or their comfort. The "club room" i.e. the room set aside for the use of club members, was actually the smokers' lounge, because the main bar was a no smoking area (this was in the days when you could still smoke indoors). Being a reformed smoker, I didn't like drinking in a room that smelt like an old ashtray. Consequently, the members tended not to hang around after a game and went home instead, which meant there was hardly any social side to the golf.

At another hotel course not far from me, if a hotel guest wishes to play golf, they are given priority on the course. It doesn't matter if the members or visitors have booked a tee time, the hotel guests will always be allowed out first. On one occasion I was playing there with our local society, which had booked several months earlier, when a half dozen hotel guests were allowed out on the course ahead of us. Clearly half of them had never held a golf club in their lives before. Six hours it took us to complete our round (the norm is around 4 to 4½ hours). What was worse, however, was when we got back to the "club house", we were told the meal we had booked wasn't ready and we would have to wait another hour! Needless to say, we didn't go back the next year.

Finally, there are the municipal and "pay to play" courses. I mention municipal courses under "dress code" so I won't cover the same ground here. Suffice to say, if these courses have a "membership" system at all it is usually just a way of offering regular visitors a discounted green fee for payment up front. There is usually no committee structure, so no one to organise competitions or social activities. Course conditions vary wildly, because the owners may decide to spend the profits on things other than course maintenance. This is especially true of municipal courses, where the owner is the local council and may take the golf club profits to pay for street lighting. Not that there's anything wrong with street lighting, but golf courses need continual investment if they are to attract golfers.

Given that golf club membership fees usually represent a considerable cash investment, it is wise to choose your golf club with care. You will probably be there for at least a year and that is a long time to be playing golf with people you don't really like.

Because it is the members who actually make a club.

* **Editor's note**: This book is being edited during the Covid-19 outbreak and the question of survival of golf clubs is again a hot topic amongst golfers. There are some real bargains to be had as clubs seek to attract new members, so it has never been a better time to take up golf.

GUR

To golfers a GUR sign is what the "Get Out of Jail Free" card is in a game of Monopoly. If their golf ball lands in an area designated as GUR, the golfer gets free relief (see *Relief*), which usually means dropping the ball in a position that is far easier to play from.

The initials mean "ground under repair". In truth it doesn't have to be actually under repair, it just means that the area concerned is being protected for some reason. It could even mean that a rare plant has been found there and is being protected from harm. It is often used where fresh turf has been laid to repair previous damage and will also be used in areas where grass has been freshly seeded or new trees planted.

As I write, in the middle of January 2020, there is a large area of our 13th hole that is roped off and marked as GUR because the ground is saturated and the club doesn't want it being churned up. So the ground to the sides is being churned up instead as golfers go around the affected area.

That is a particular circumstance, of course, but parts of the course may be designated GUR for many reasons. A golf ball landing on a mole hill, for example, is covered by a specific rule and relief may be taken. But an area where there are several mole hills close together may be designated as GUR because trying to take relief becomes too difficult, with the ball likely to still be affected regardless of where it may be dropped. Poorly maintained bunkers are often designated GUR until greenkeepers have the time (and money) to get around to sorting them out. I have played at one course (which will remain nameless) where all the bunkers on the course were designated GUR because of maintenance issues.

I have just one story relating to GUR. My ball having landed in an area designated as such, I took my free relief and lined up my next shot. A small metal sign used to designate the area as GUR was stuck in the ground directly in front of me, but I decided not to move it because, after all, the likelihood of me hitting it was infinitesimally small (you may already be ahead of me here). I struck the ball a mighty blow, it shot forward, hit the metal sign and rose skywards to land ten yards behind me. So not only did my shot count, my next shot would count as well and I also had to make it from further back from the hole.

That's golf for you! And it was also another example of poor course management.

H is For

Hacker

What most amateurs are when they start out. As the word suggests, it means hacking at the golf course with a club, raising divots and doing damage. Some golfers grow out of being a hacker, some never do and some return to hacking in later life.

People who never get away from being hackers often give up the game in frustration. Which is a shame because a few lessons would probably have got them past their problems.

Halfway House

A place halfway (approximately) around a golf course where you could buy refreshments if it was open, but it isn't because of staff shortages, insufficient demand or because nobody remembered to open it up. The best halfway houses, if open, serve alcohol.

If it is open it offers the chance to take a short pause from golf.

If you pass the clubhouse between the 9th and 10th holes, then the halfway house is the same as the Nineteenth Hole (see *Nineteenth Hole*) if you can nip in to buy something without needing to remove your golf shoes.

Some halfway houses just contain vending machines which take your money but refuse to dispense your purchase. Coffee or tea served from these vending machines, if they work, is usually undrinkable, but you buy it anyway because it's hot and you're cold.

Handicap

Despite its long history, handicaps were only introduced into golf in the UK in 1911. The purpose is to allow golfers of differing standards to play in the same competitions on a more equal footing. As a pretty average golfer I couldn't hope to take on a good golfer without the benefit of my handicap. Unless he had the worst round of his life and I had my best round ever, he would be bound to win.

But with my handicap of 23 and his, perhaps, of 5 we deduct one from the other and it means he has to "give me" 18 strokes. That is a stroke on very hole. So if he scores a par I can score a bogey and we "halve" the hole. If I also score a par (not entirely unknown) I would win the hole. If I can win more holes than my opponent, I win the match.

Various surveys have found that the average handicap for male golfers is 14.3 and for women is 26.5. One survey, conducted by Golf Digest, also showed that men's handicaps have reduced by 2 strokes since 1991 and those for women by nearly 3. This may be as a consequence of improved technology in the sport, or perhaps we are all just getting better at the game.

First, how do you get a handicap? Well, in most cases, you have to be a member of a golf club. This is because the award of a handicap is an integral part of the game and has to be governed accordingly. Golf clubs are required to manage the handicaps of their members and will usually have a committee member appointed to carry out that task. This means that when golfers from different clubs play in the same competitions, they should all be playing on a level playing field (I know they play on a golf course. Don't be so literal!).

In November 2020 the World Handicapping System (WHS) is to be introduced, which will formalise this globally and golf clubs will be required to submit data on course length, difficulty and player performance to ensure that their members' handicaps are correct.

The usual way to get a handicap is to submit three scorecards which have been witnessed by another club member (some clubs insist on one of the rounds being witnessed by a committee member). The aggregate score from those three rounds of golf will be taken and used to calculate the golfer's handicap. Until 2018 the maximum handicap for men was 28, but this has now been increased to 54. It is also 54 for women golfers. The purpose of the change was to encourage more people to take up the game. There is little evidence that this has worked as very few non-golfers know about the change.

What does all that mean in practical terms? Well, let's say I play 90 shots during a round of golf. That is my "gross" score. My handicap today is 23, so I deduct 23 from 90 to give me a "nett" score of 67. All the people entered into the same competition will have their nett scores ranked, low to high, to decide who has won.

However, even taking handicaps into account it can be expected that the better golfers, those with lower handicaps, will still win more competitions than those with higher handicaps. For this reason, most clubs divide their members up into divisions based on handicaps. Typically the divisions will be:

Handicap of 10 or lower - Division 1.
Handicap of 11 to 18 - Division 2.
Handicap of over 18 - Division 3.

However, divisions are a matter of local policy and it's up to the club how many divisions to have and where they set the break points.

Most monthly medals are competed for on a divisional basis, so there will be a winner and a runner-up in each division.

With handicaps of up to 54 now allowed, we can probably expect to see more divisions being introduced as golfers whose previous handicaps were 28 start to head upwards towards the new maximum. For our seniors' section we have two divisions, the dividing line being a handicap of 18. That is because handicaps tend to head north as you get older, so we don't have enough golfers on a sub 10 handicap to make it worthwhile putting them in a division of their own.

Handicaps are adjusted whenever a golfer plays in a "qualifying" competition. In real terms this means any competition where the golfer's individual score can be identified and counted, however, during the winter there may be no qualifying competitions, or at least very few. Course conditions have to be taken into account, as does player performance on the day. It would be rather unfair to make a big adjustment to a golfer's handicap just because they had one exceptional round in a run of otherwise mediocre performances.

In addition, all golf clubs carry out an annual review of handicaps. This will incorporate all of a golfer's recorded scores to take into account their general standard of play. This helps to prevent golfers protecting their handicap by only playing in "non-qualifying" competitions.

Handicaps and handicapping has always been viewed as something of a "dark art" and this is why the topic is one of the more frequent and noisy ones discussed in the bar after games.

If a player is fortunate enough to win a few competitions in a short space of time (or is perceived to have) then the first thing some other golfers will attack is their handicap. It is rarely justified, as the modern computerised scoring systems will always make the necessary adjustments within the handicapping rules. If the golfer has been protecting their handicap, this will be discovered during the annual review but, of course, waiting until the end of the year before seeing an adjustment to the accused golfer's handicap isn't satisfactory for some golfers, despite the rules on handicapping laying out precisely how it should all be done.

Despite the changes to the handicapping rules and system, I think I can safely say that handicaps will remain a hot topic in golf clubs for a long time to come. Even the new handicapping rules (see *Slope System*) being introduced under the WHS won't stop some people griping about the handicaps of others.

One of the things that is known about the WHS is that handicaps will, in future, be based on the golfer's best 8 rounds from their last 20. This means that the handicap is based on actual performance, rather than potential performance. If a golfer is having a run of bad form, it could take up to 13 poor rounds before their handicap is adjusted upwards, but only one good round for it to be adjusted downwards.

Committees will also be able to insert "penalty scores" for golfers who don't return a score for a competition, or who are DQ'd. That prevents people from protecting their handicap by not returning a score or by failing to sign their card. The penalty score will always be the equivalent to the best round from the previous 20.

There are a few mythical golfers who have a negative handicap. That means that they are better than "scratch" (see *Scratch*). To calculate their nett score they actually have to add strokes on after the round, rather than deduct them. How harsh is that?

Hardened aircraft shelter

A hardened aircraft shelter (HAS) is not something that most golfers, amateur or otherwise, will ever encounter on a golf course. I include it only to illustrate how great the variations in golf courses can be.

I first took up the game of golf in the late 1980s while serving in the RAF in Germany, at a base called RAF Laarbruch. Until then I had played rugby, but my age was starting to tell on me and my body could no longer tolerate the battering it was receiving on the rugby pitch, so I needed a new outlet for my energies.

Being a base that might be attacked by the air forces of Soviet Russia, all the aircraft at Laarbruch (Tornado bombers at that time) were housed in HASs. Theoretically these were bomb proof, even if they took a direct hit.

On the base we had a nine hole golf course which was maintained by the members themselves. No taxpayers' money could be spent on something as frivolous as golf. A couple of the holes were quite close to a HAS that was sited in a part of the airfield called Blue Sector, which 15 Squadron called home. (This is all just scene setting) It was a local rule that you weren't permitted to play those holes if the HAS doors were open or if there was an aircraft parked outside it, for fear of damaging a very expensive bit of taxpayer funded property (a Tornado cost about £17 million. A pittance compared with the new F35s that are just coming into service). Even with the HAS doors open, the dark interior made it difficult to see if there was an aircraft inside, hence the need for the rule.

But when the HAS doors were closed and there were no parked aircraft, you could play those holes.

I was a novice golfer. I was teeing up my next shot. I checked to see if the HAS doors were shut. They were.

I took a mighty swing and saw my ball arc off to the right, directly towards the HAS. You have no idea how hard a golf ball will bounce off pre-stressed reinforced concrete until you have seen one hit a HAS. I'm sure it flew off faster than it had hit, if that is possible. It was a sight to behold.

Needless to say, the ball was never seen again. So when you see your ball hit a tree, think how fortunate you are not to have to contend with HASs as well.

The 9th and final hole ran parallel to a taxiway, the route taken by aircraft to get to and from the runway. Another local rule stipulated that you couldn't play that hole if an aircraft was using the taxiway, nor could you cross the taxiway to retrieve errant balls. With the air traffic control tower sited just beyond the 9th green you could be sure that any breaches of the rules would be spotted and the culprit taken to task.

This wasn't just a matter of getting a telling off or incurring a penalty shot. The rules were stipulated in "Standing Orders" which made it a serious disciplinary matter if they were broken.

I hit the longest drive I have ever hit on that hole. My ball struck the taxiway, bounced along its hard surface for a couple of hundred yards, struck a light fitting and returned obediently to the fairway just short of the green. According to the scorecard I had just hit a drive of about 350 yards. Ah, the joys of golf.

It is worthy of note that the longest distance a golf ball has ever been hit is 657 yards, along the concrete runway of RAF Honington in Suffolk, during a special event to commemorate the 100th anniversary of the RAF.

As an aside, if you ever fly Ryanair into Weeze* (pronounced Vay-tsah) Airport, formerly known as RAF Laarbruch, you will still see those HASs. If a Russian bomb (or a golf ball) can't demolish them, then nothing else can, unless you also want to demolish a sizeable portion of western Germany and eastern Netherlands. Sadly, the golf course wasn't so robust and has been reclaimed by nature.

* Ryanair calls this Dusseldorf (Weeze) Airport. The distance from Weeze Airport to downtown Dusseldorf by road is 82 km (approx 50 miles) and the journey takes 55 minutes. It's about double that travelling time by train. Just so you know before you book.

Hazards

There are two types of hazard, bunkers and water. Both are covered under their own headings.

Try not to end up in either.

Technically, since 2019 hazards no longer exist. You won't find them in the definitions contained in the rules of golf. Now they are defined either as "penalty areas" or bunkers. I'm not sure if that makes them easier to understand or not.

Penalty areas, however, come in two forms. Form 1 is any area of water (other than temporary water) and form 2 is any area that the committee decides is a penalty area.

Penalty areas can also be changed. A ditch that has water in it during the winter may be marked as a penalty area but may be changed to "general area" in the summer when it is dry.

You don't have to take the penalty, though. If your ball is half in and half out of the water, you can play it without penalty if you fancy your chances. This rarely ends well (see *Course management*) and is one of the reasons why golfers carry towels..

Head

As in, keeping your head down. Moving the head before the point when the golf club strikes the ball is the most common cause of a bad shot. Its origins are in the desire to see what happens to the shot before the shot has actually been made, but knowing that doesn't stop the golfer from doing it.

It is most commonly experienced amongst the ranks of the beginners, but seasoned golfers are also quite likely to do it, especially when making a tricky shot.

The fastest route to becoming a millionaire would be to invent a device that will keep a golfer's head stationary over the ball until the club head has struck it. I await your suggestions with bated breath.

Hole-in-one

Many, many pros never achieve this feat, but I have and so have many other amateurs. Essentially, anyone can score a hole-in-one, so long as they are capable of hitting a ball in the right direction.

The odds against scoring a hole-in-one are 12,500 to 1 for an amateur and 2,500 to 1 for a professional. The odds for the pro are shorter mainly because they play so many rounds of golf each year. The more shots you hit, the more likely it is that one will find the target.

By tradition it is quite expensive to achieve a hole-in-one as the beneficiary is expected to buy a round of drinks for everyone in the clubhouse bar. In some clubs they put a bottle of whisky or brandy on the bar for the members to help themselves and the beneficiary replaces it at cost price.

To protect against the financial implications of scoring a hole-in-one, most golf insurance policies will pay out a cash sum on production of a certified scorecard or a letter from the club Secretary.

There is various paraphernalia that can be purchased to celebrate this achievement, such as hole-in-one ties or cufflinks, framed certificates etc. There are a couple of websites where you can register your achievement for posterity. Some golf clubs have their own hole-in-one honours board (though mine, sadly, doesn't).

Hole out

To complete the hole by putting the ball into the hole. If a putt is conceded by an opponent in match play or "social golf" there is no need to hole out, but in stroke play and stableford (see *Stableford*) competitions, it is a requirement.

Honours board

Boards used to decorate the walls of golf clubs where the winners of major club trophies (see *Trophies*) are listed.

Honours boards are usually accompanied by one of the trophies that are displayed in the clubhouse. If you want your name to be remembered once you have passed on to that great golf club in the sky, winning a major competition and getting your name on an honours board is one way of ensuring it.

Yes, my name is on an honours board at my club - four actually and one of them twice.

Hugs

There isn't much room in golf for hugs, other than for tournament winners hugging their spouse or partner. But this incident a few days ago prompted me to put it in.

I was playing a round with a bloke who had his sone with him, both travelling in a buggy. The lad was about 7 or 8 years old and spent most of his time on a portable games console thingy (I'm not technical).

Dad hit an unusually bad shot and sent his ball out of bounds, to which the lad responded "Was that a bad shot day?"

To which dad replied, "yes son, it was a bad shot."

The boy then said "Would a hug help?

So, to Anthony, the little boy who wants to hug his dad when he hits a bad shot, this entry is dedicated.

I is For

Insurance

In this litigious age it is recommended that amateurs take out golf insurance. This can cover a multitude of eventualities from third party injuries to the loss of golf clubs and other equipment through theft and, as mentioned above, the cost of scoring a hole-in-one.

Golf insurance isn't expensive. Mine costs me about £45 ($50) a year and has done for many years. Given that the damages awarded for injuring someone could run into millions of pounds, plus legal fees, the risk of not having insurance far outweighs the cost of having it.

You can look up "golf insurance" on line, or ask in your pro shop. They probably have a tie in to a golf insurance provider. You can also look on the England Golf website (see "Sources" at the end of the book) as they have a partnership arrangement with an insurance company.

"In the Hole"

A phrase shouted by moronic spectators at televised golf tournaments, in the hope of hearing their own voice when they play back the recording when they get home.

Irons

So called because the club head is made of "iron". They are actually made of steel, but "steels" doesn't sound right. See *Clubs*.

There are two basic types of iron that can be purchased. For low handicap amateurs and the professionals there are "blades". These are clubs with a smooth profile where all the power of the club is focused into one area of the club's face, known as the "sweet spot". Connecting the sweet spot with the ball is always going to produce good results. But that is harder to do for the amateur as there is very little margin of error.

The amateur, therefore, tends to favour cavity backed clubs. These have a larger head with solid rim but a hollow back, which makes the whole head more of a sweet spot which, in turn, makes the club easier to use. However, the cavity reduces the amount of power transferred from the club head to the ball and therefore cavity backed clubs sacrifice distance for ease of use.

J is For

Jargon

Perhaps because the game of golf is so old, it has spawned more jargon and slang than any other. At least, that's how it seems to me. In terms of fashion, jargon comes and goes. Changes to the rules also affect the use of jargon. For example, the word "stymie". This word has translated into the general language as some sort of problem that can't be overcome. A crossword aficionado might refer to being "stymied" by a difficult clue. But it originated in golf.

It means to have your putt blocked by another ball between you and the hole, such that you can't putt in a straight line. You have to go around the ball in front, which means having to take two putts instead of one. The origins are no doubt Scottish and it certainly has that sort of feel to the word.

But you can no longer be stymied in golf, because the rules changed several decades ago to allow a player to ask the owner of the blocking ball to lift it and mark the place where it was, thereby allowing a straight putt at the hole. If the ball marker itself is still in the way, the person putting can ask for it to be moved to one side. So, no more stymies in golf, but they still exist in crosswords and other insurmountable puzzles.

There is a Wikipedia page (see sources) which list all these terms, so I'm not going to go into detail on them, you may hear them on the golf course and you may not, but they aren't vital knowledge. I have included a lot of the jargon that is still in use in this A to Z, but here's a sample of some others that you can look up if you want: Ambrose, artisan, dog licence, ferret, gimme, mashie, moving day, Nassau, pop-up, Rowan, sandbagging, snowman, turkey, worm-burner, zinger.

Jokes

A four-ball takes between four and five hours to complete a typical round of golf. Less than an hour of that is actually spent striking the ball, which leaves between three and four hours of other activity. Aside from walking, talking is what fills much of that time.

As with evenings in the pub, the telling of jokes is very much a part of talking when on the golf course. If the jokes are golf related, so much the better, but they don't have to be.

I'm not going to launch into a series of jokes here. Most of the ones I know are so familiar even non-golfers will have heard them before. If you want to read a few golfing jokes, there are books you can buy and whole websites dedicated to them.

The nature of the jokes told over time has changed considerably. In the UK, the game was once the bastion of the white middle class male, so the jokes reflected that. Fortunately the world has moved on and the subjects of jokes are more broadly based and a little less likely to cause offence. There is still a thread of misogyny running through golfing jokes, much as some comedians still tell "mother-in-law" jokes, but even that, thankfully, is starting to disappear.

The mainstay of the golfing joke is the bad golfer and there is a whole website dedicated to that subject. I will quote just one:

Q: What is the difference between a lost golf ball and the G-spot?
A: A man will spend three minutes looking for the lost golf ball.

I said it was a joke, I didn't say it was a funny joke! Actually, that joke had to be updated in 2019 when rule 18.2a reduced the time permitted to search for a ball from five minutes to three. It was probably funnier at five minutes, but more accurate at three.

K is For

Kill the ball

To hit the ball with considerable aggression. This usually results in a poor shot and is accompanied by much swearing when the shot goes wrong.

L is For

Lay up

What most amateurs wish they had done right after their ball has landed in a water hazard or bunker.

To lay up is to play a shot deliberately short in order to avoid ending up in trouble. To do so always sacrifices distance, which is why amateurs so often choose not to do it. The lay-up shot is a tool in course management.

If a golfer miscues a shot then claims it was a deliberate lay up, it is considered bad form to laugh or tell him he was lying.

Learning to play

The best way to learn to play golf is to start at the age of five. But if it is already too late for that (if you are five then congratulations on your reading ability) take lessons from a professional. They have coaching qualifications and can point out the best way to hold a club, stand, swing the club etc. But professionals cost money, so many golfers either take lessons from an unqualified amateur, or they just pitch up on the course and hack away, learning as they go.

Not surprisingly, because it isn't nearly as easy as the pros make it look, this results in a poor experience for the golfer and they often abandon the game before they really get started. Even if they go onto the driving range to learn, the results will be the same, because they start out with their driver, which is the hardest club in the bag to master. If they started out differently, they might have a better experience and come to love the game.

Learning from other amateurs sometimes works, but often the novice is just taught the bad habits of their tutor and so will never develop further than their tutor has. If the tutor is a high handicapper, then the novice will probably also never be anything other than a high handicapper.

If you want to go it alone, it has been suggested to me that the following sequence is used to learn to play the game.

Putting. Firstly, you can teach yourself this at home, on your living room carpet, putting into a mug that's lying on its side. Secondly you can just turn up at many golf clubs and use their putting green for free; all you need is one ball and a putter. Start close to the hole and move further away as you start to become successful. Also start on a flat bit of the putting green (this shouldn't be an issue at home unless you have a badly built house), then move on to holes with slopes so you can learn to "read the green". (**Publisher's note**: No liability is accepted for damage caused while practicing at home.)

Chipping. This is a shot played from the side of the green intended to get the ball close to the hole. Really it is just a putting stroke using a club with a "lofted" face which will lift the ball out of the grass and deposit it on the green. It is a skill that will pay dividends later in terms of scoring.

Pitching. The first club you need to go onto a driving range to learn how to use. This is an extension of chipping, usually designed to get the ball over a bunker or other hazard. A pitching wedge throws the ball high into the air to land on the green and stop. Another skill that will save many strokes on the score card once mastered.

Irons. Irons are used far more often than woods and are easier to learn how to use. Start with a nine iron and work your way through the numbers. Some golfers never use woods because they have developed such skill with their irons that they don't need them, especially on shorter courses such as the one where I play.

<u>Woods</u>. If you don't get lessons on how to use any other club, get them for learning how to use woods. The length of their shafts make them difficult to use and frustrating to master. But if you do decide not to get lessons, be patient and make sure you take a very slow backswing.

But I do recommend getting lessons from a pro as being the best and least frustrating way to learn the game. Most pros sell vouchers for a set number of lessons, so put them on your Christmas list. Six half hour sessions will get you started.

Please don't use sports fields or playing fields to learn how to play golf. It damages the ground and lost balls (and you will lose them) become a hazard to others. Dogs swallow lost balls and other sports people tread on them and lose their footing or fall on them and injure themselves.

Links

Golf probably takes up more ground per person playing than any other game. Therefore, the spread and development of the sport was dependent on land being available on which it could be played.

For the landed gentry this was no problem. They could build a private golf course on their own land and invite their friends to play. But if a group of people in a town wanted to the play the game, it wasn't viable because of the price of land. The only real option was to play on "common land" but that was usually being used for grazing animals. With the advent of several "enclosures acts", much of what was once common land was lost to avaricious landowners.

In the UK and especially Scotland there was, however, one source of land that was cheap. It was cheap because it couldn't be used for anything else.

Between the sea and the more usable land there was often a series of sand dunes, built up by the actions of tide, waves and wind. Grass found it difficult to grow, which meant it was of no use for grazing sheep or cattle; crops wouldn't grow on it and its soft and shifting nature made it unsuitable for building houses. These dunes "linked" the useable land to the sea but had no other purpose as far as most people were concerned.

Most of this land was owned by the Crown, who didn't really want it either, so a group of golfers could club together to buy the land quite cheaply and develop it as a golf course and the "golf links" was born.

The shape of the course was dictated by the area covered by the dunes. For this reason links courses tend to spread along the coastline, but are quite narrow. They also varied in size. Some had as few as six holes, while others had more than twenty. At this time there was no "standard" number of holes for a course, so the number of holes on the course didn't really matter. There weren't any written rules for golf until the Gentlemen Golfers of Leith wrote down some for the Edinburgh Silver Cup in 1744 (probably the first set of written rules for any sport and more 100 years older than those for football, rugby and tennis). Neither did the boundaries of the course matter too much. I have seen photographs of Victorian ladies in their crinolines playing shots from a rocky beach. Now that's one heck of a bunker to play out of.

As time went on and the golf clubs that emerged were able to attract more income, they were able to import topsoil which improved the fairways and the greens. Particular sand loving grasses were planted that stabilised the sand dunes and the links course became a thing of beauty.

Also with greater income came the ability to buy neighbouring land, which allowed smaller courses to expand.

St Andrews, itself a links course, is accepted as the world home of golf, but at one time it had twenty two holes. In 1764 this was reduced to eighteen. The following record of the decision exists:

"St. Andrews 4th October 1764.

The captain and gentlemen golfers, are of (the) opinion, that it would be for the improvement of the links, that the four first holes should be converted into two. They therefore have agreed that for the future, they shall be played as two holes, in the same way as presently marked out.

Wm. St Claire (William St. Claire, Club Captain)"

Over time eighteen holes became the standard as other clubs sought to emulate the R&A. If a course didn't have eighteen holes, they would play whatever they had in a combination that added up to eighteen. Courses with more than eighteen holes reduced the number, often by combining holes to add to their length, as St Andrews had done.

Although "The Open" is recognised as the oldest international golf tournament in the world, it was originally played on a twelve hole course at Prestwick. It wasn't played over eighteen holes until it went to Muirfield in 1891 (home of the Gentlemen Golfers of Leith, who had now become the Honourable Company of Edinburgh Golfers). It is one of the defining features of The Open that it is always played on a links course.

Links courses offer unique challenges for the amateur; at least for those amateurs who aren't fortunate enough to be members of a links golf club in the first place.

The slopes of the ground mean that the golfer is never standing on a flat surface. That means that the ball is usually either above or below the golfer's feet. Non-golfers won't understand what that means in practical terms, but basically, it makes any shot much harder to control.

The greens are also different. Not only are they grown from a different type of grass, which affects their texture, but they undulate in some eccentric ways. There is no such thing as a flat green on a links course and therefore no such thing as a simple putt. Putting can be something of a lottery, as even the greatest professional golfers have discovered during The Open.

Finally there is the weather. As links courses are, by definition, on the coast there is hardly ever a day when the wind isn't blowing. I have played in a howling gale only to be told by a club member that it was only a mild breeze! "You should be here when the wind really gets up." He said.

No thanks!

There are two blessings for links courses. The first is that there are very few, if any, trees (see *Trees*) to get in the way. The second is that their sandy base allows the course to drain very well, which means they usually have good playing conditions all year round.

But on one thing almost all amateurs can agree, playing on a links course is a true test of a golfer's ability, which is why so many amateurs travel to Scotland to play them. But please don't dismiss Ireland, which also has some great links courses.

My own favourite links course is in Co Donegal in Ireland; a small country golf club called Portsalon. Not only is it a lovely course, but some of its holes offer the most spectacular views over the neighbouring sea loch. The locals are friendly as well.

Local rules

Despite their best efforts, the R&A can't think of everything when it comes to rules. In particular they can't be aware of the specific features of every golf course and take those into account when devising the RoG. To compensate for that, golf clubs are allowed to compile their own local rules.

Local rules may not contradict the RoG, however they may modify them in light of local conditions. They are usually printed on the rear of the scorecard, so it is worthwhile, when playing an unfamiliar course, for the amateur to turn the scorecard over and have a read of them. They may save the golfer a stroke here or there.

There are three areas which can be covered by local rules. These are:

- Defining course boundaries and other areas of the course,
- Defining special or required relief areas.
- Defining abnormal course conditions and integral objects.

You would think that defining the boundaries of a golf course would be a simple matter, but there are sometimes complications. On our course, for example, there is a series of out-of-bounds (see *Out of bounds*) markers along a line between the 1st and the 18th holes, effectively creating a "boundary" within the course itself. To complicate matters, if you cross the line from the 1st, you aren't out of bounds but if you cross the line from the 18th, you are.

If the logic of that escapes you, it wouldn't if you were standing on the course. Standing on the 1st tee you have the clubhouse behind you and you are hitting away from it. But standing on the 18th tee you are hitting towards the clubhouse, about two thirds of the way along the fairway on the right.

So, if your shot leaks to the right from the 18th tee and you end up on the 1st fairway, you might be tempted to play your next shot over the clubhouse roof to get back onto the 18th fairway again, risking broken windows or hitting golfers practicing on the putting green which is hidden from view by the building. In addition, next to the clubhouse is a marquee which is used to host wedding receptions and the wedding guests often gather on the lawn between the marquee and the clubhouse on nice days. Flying golf balls can kill and no one wants to ruin the bride's big day by killing one of her guests. The bride herself will be fine as she will have so much hairspray applied that it will act like a crash helmet.

You may think that nobody would be stupid enough to attempt a shot such as that. You would be wrong. I have had to speak to one visitor to tell them they were out of bounds and shouldn't be playing from where they were and I know that other members have had to do the same.

So, our local rules point out that the out of bounds markers are (1) there and (2) only apply if you are approaching from a certain direction.

Because a golf ball can end up literally anywhere on the course, it is necessary to indicate in local rules where you may get special relief and where you must take a penalty if you need to take relief.

For example, if the owner of the club has just planted a whole lot of new trees, they don't want them all being hacked down by golfers trying to get back to the fairway. So they may specify that you can have free relief if you are in a plantation, or from trees shorter than a certain height (typically two club lengths). The rule will also specify where that relief may be taken. Similarly, local rules often allow relief to be taken from trees that are supported by a stake or a tube, even if they are taller than the designated height.

If there is a water hazard then the club may wish to specify an area where the ball may be dropped, referred to as a "drop zone", so that all golfers who land in the water play their next shot from the same place. This is common in professional golf tournaments but is sometimes seen elsewhere.

The committee decides on local rules and their application, but they may not change or waive any penalty. To get around that, they have to change the designation of objects around the course. They may, for example, rule that a bunker is GUR because its condition has deteriorated. This will allow the golfer to lift their ball out of the bunker without incurring a penalty, which would not normally be allowed.

On our course we have three wooden huts, provided to shelter golfers in the event of a thunderstorm, where it is too far for them to retreat to the clubhouse if the storm breaks while they are on the course. If a golfer's ball ends up behind one of those huts, they will have a problem playing their next shot. So, on our course, the huts are covered by a local rule that defines them as immoveable obstructions and relief may be taken under the relevant rule. The local rule also specifies how far the ball can be moved before it has to be dropped.

So local rules can be very beneficial and are worth reading.

Lost Ball

Even pros lose the odd ball, though given the presence of spectators on the course they do it far less often than amateurs. The spectators act as their unpaid "forecaddies".

In truth, no ball is ever lost, it is only misplaced or mislaid. I know this to be true because on pretty much every round of golf I play I find a ball lying somewhere that has clearly been mislaid. In some cases, I find myself asking "How could they possibly have missed seeing that?" In most such cases it was because the golfers were looking in the wrong area thinking the ball had travelled further than it had (They rarely assume it has gone a shorter distance).

Naturally, for such a common occurrence the RoG are quite clear on the penalties to be applied and the way to proceed with the game. Put simply, once it has been agreed with your partners that the ball is, indeed, lost you return to the place from which you last played, you drop a replacement ball and play another shot. When it comes to counting up the score for the hole, you include the original shot (the one that resulted in the ball being lost), the shot taken with the replacement ball and add a one shot penalty.

Lost balls are one of the main reasons for slow play.

Firstly the golfer is allowed only three minutes (it used to be five) to search for their ball. The thing is, I have never seen any golfer look at his watch to start timing the three minutes. Neither have I ever seen them check the time to see how much has elapsed. The general impetus for them to move on is the appearance of the group behind them, ready to play their shots.

Secondly, many golfers help a partner to look for a lost ball before starting to look for their own. This can result in not three minutes being lost, but six, nine or even twelve (more in fact, because no one really knows how long they've been looking).

To keep the game moving, find your own ball first, before helping to look for anyone else's. If your own ball is not easily visible leave a marker, such as your golf bag or trolley, so you can find it again. On more than one occasion I have found my own ball, gone to help someone else find theirs and then returned to where I thought my ball was only to discover I couldn't find it again. Embarrassing.

Finally, if in doubt about where your ball may have ended up, play a provisional ball (see *Provisional ball*).

Technically speaking any ball found on a golf course belongs to the golf course owners, not to the person who found it. Just a legal point, in case you ever have to defend yourself on the matter.

It is polite to wait for a ball to stop moving before "finding" it. In other words, don't assume it has been lost. It may just have come from a golfer playing a different hole and they are going to be mighty displeased when their ball can't be found. I know, it happened to me.

There is a golf course in Milton Keynes, where I once played, where kids from the local housing estate run onto the fairway (they can't be seen from the tee) and nick the golf balls as they roll down the hill. One of my partners actually chased them through the houses to get his ball back. That took them by surprise! But I don't suppose it stopped them doing it.

Looking for a lost ball.

M is For

Match play

This is the form of golf where players play "head to head" and hole by hole. It is the usual form for knock-out competitions and for matches against other golf clubs.

Basically, the lowest score on each hole wins the hole. When a golfer has won more holes than there are remaining to play, he has won the match. For example, if the golfer has a lead of three holes and there are only two holes left to play, he is said to have won by 3 & 2. Once a winning margin has been established the players aren't required to complete the remaining holes, but it is often the case that these are played out for "fun". It isn't that much fun if you happen to be the loser.

Obviously, handicaps have to be taken into account, so the player with the higher handicap (say 23) deducts the handicap of the lower golfer (say 18) to leave 5. This is how many extra strokes the higher handicap player will receive from the lower handicap player during the round. He will get one those strokes at each of the five most difficult holes as detailed by the Stroke Index (see *Stroke index*) indicated on the score card.

So, if the lower handicap player scores a par on a hole and the higher handicap player scores a bogey, but has an extra stoke allowed on that hole, the hole will be "halved" or shared.

This format can also be played in pairs. In that case the "best ball" wins the hole. That is to say the player amongst the four who has the best score, taking their handicap allowance into account, wins the hole for their pair. In pairs golf the handicap allowance is usually 90% of the calculated difference, rather than 100%. This takes into account that there are two players on each team, so there is an increased chance of one of them having a good score.

In knock-out competitions, if there is a tie after 18 holes, the golfers will have a sudden death play-off over the holes that have been designated for the purpose. These needn't be holes that are sequential on the scorecard, but may be any holes that are detailed in the competition rules. Typically, they will be holes close to the clubhouse. Any handicap allowance that was applied when the holes were originally played will be allowed again during the play-off.

When played as a team game, one golf club against another, each match is awarded one point for a win and half a point for a draw. The team with the most points after all the matches have been completed is the winning team. In the event of a tie, the winning margins for each match are added together and the team with the higher score is the winner. So, if one team wins three of its matches by 3&2, 4&3 and by a single hole, their score is 8. If their opponents score less than 8, they lose. In friendly matches the two teams usually settle for a draw if that was the original result.

Members

It is members who make a club and who also make it a pleasure to become a member at a club. But if you are joining a club for the first time, or even moving from one club to another, don't expect too much in one go.

Clubs of any sort are often accused of being "cliquey", of not welcoming new members in or even of shutting them out. It is unfortunate, but for golf clubs there is a bit of a reason.

If Fred, Charlie, Terry and Dan have been playing the same four-ball at 8.15 on Sunday morning for the last twenty years, they are not going to kick a pal out of the group to make way for a new member. That may make them seem unwelcoming, but hey - would you ditch a mate just because someone new has appeared on the scene? (I'm guessing that some readers may now be saying "depends on the mate".)

The way to establish a friendly circle at a new club is to enter competitions.

Most clubs display a "sign-up" sheet for their competitions. Look for the empty slots and put your name down. Immediately you will get to know two or three members when you go out to play in the competition with them. Make sure you stay for a drink afterwards, rather than running off home straight away. It shows that you are willing to be sociable.

Do that for a few weeks and you will soon build up a circle of acquaintances and they may well invite you to join them when Terry is on holiday or Dan has to go and visit his old Mum.

The other way of establishing yourself is to seek out other new members and offer to make up a group with them. You may establish your own regular four-ball that will play together for the next twenty years. If not, at least you know a few more people.

Anyone who knows me knows that I am a bit of an introvert (writers often are). That means I don't actually like meeting new people. I'm happy with people I already know, but new people are scary. But I adopted both approaches described above and I now have regular partners for when I play golf - and they aren't new, scary people, they are on now old pals and aren't scary at all (well, maybe Helmut is a bit scary but that's a separate issue).

Membership fees

All golf clubs charge a fee to be a member. Municipal courses (owned by the local council, but sometimes franchised out) may not do that, in which case they are known as "pay to play" courses. But assuming the course where you want to join does have members, you will have to pay a membership fee.

There were, at one time, many clubs that charged a "joining fee" as well. That got you through the clubhouse doors, but you still had to pay an annual membership fee on top. Joining fees are less common than they used to be because competition has driven them out. Joining fees are a way of restricting membership to those who can afford to pay and the sorts of clubs that still charge them also often have waiting lists to join.

So, how much can you expect to pay? Well, for my club they vary from around £700 to just under £1,000 depending on age. If that sounds like a lot of money, I should warn you that we are at the cheaper end of the market. Membership fees in excess of £1,000 are common and at the very top end you can expect to add an extra zero.

Whether you think the membership fee offers value for money or not is a matter of personal judgement. Comparing the cost with what it would cost me if I paid a green fee every time I played on a Saturday during the summer months, shows that I break even somewhere around the 25th round of golf. As I play about 80 rounds of golf a year, I am clearly in profit. I have, however, heard of golfers whose rounds work out at £400 each because they've paid their membership fee then hardly ever played golf that year,

Because of the expense, many clubs offer staggered payment systems, such as monthly payment by direct debit. They also offer reduced fees for members who only want to play on weekdays (5 day memberships as they are called), which are less busy. Some courses also operate systems whereby you can buy a number of "points" which are then used up each time you visit the course. When you run out of points you can buy more.

A good time to go looking for deals on annual memberships is towards the end of the membership year, say the last 3 to 4 months. Clubs will often offer a fifteen or sixteen month membership at a reduced rate just to attract new members before they can join other clubs in the area. It's worth knowing what the membership year is for all the clubs in your area so you can keep a lookout for deals.

Finally, there are things called "country memberships", also known as "artisan memberships". These are useful for people who have holiday homes with a golf course nearby where they like to play when they visit. It allows the benefit of membership of the nearby club, without the expense of paying the full annual membership fee.

So, what do you get for your membership fee? Clearly you get unlimited golf, but you also get priority tee times. At the weekend at our club, guests and visitors aren't permitted to play before 11.00 a.m. on Saturday or Sunday to allow the members free access. You get the right to enter all competitions, which you wouldn't as a non-member and the club will also manage your handicap.

Handicap management is becoming more important these days as the World Handicap System kicks in. You won't be able to enter a competition anywhere in the world unless you have a managed handicap and some courses won't allow you to play as a visitor if you haven't got a handicap as that is proof you aren't a hacker who will ruin their course.

If you want to invite a friend to play at your club, they will usually be given a discounted green fee because you are a member and you may also get discounted rates for things like buggy hire. Finally, members often qualify for a discount on food and drink and for products bought in the pro shop as well, but the availability and amount varies from club to club.

Mental game, the

I was a going to use some inspiring lines of poetry here about keeping your head and wanting to win, but decided not to for two reasons. The first is that I'm unsure of the copyright implications and the second is that the average poet knows nothing about golf.

As with most sports, the mental game makes a considerable contribution to success or failure, particularly the latter. If you think you aren't going to make a particular shot, then it is odds on that you won't. This is especially true for putting.

It doesn't matter how many books you have read on the subject of the power of positive thinking, it will all desert you the instant you have to make a three foot putt to win (or lose) a match.

Any sports psychologists out there will probably disagree, but the vast majority of amateur golfers can't afford to pay a sports psychologist. We just have to get on with it as best we can.

It is an immutable rule of golf that immediately after birdying the most difficult hole on the golf course, you will triple bogey the next hole, which is probably the easiest (see the story of Will Reeves, told under the heading of *Albatross*). Call it hubris, call it adrenalin rush, put it in a dress and call it Mary; it doesn't matter, it will happen.

Monthly Medal

Which part of this needs explaining? It's a competition organised at golf clubs every month, the prize for which is a medal.

Mulligan

A free shot granted as a favour because the first attempt was so bad.

You will find no references to mulligans in the RoG because they aren't recognised. Actually, sometimes they are. On our 12th hole we have some electricity cables crossing above the fairway just in front of the tee. A local rule states that if your ball strikes these cables you are entitled to play the shot again without penalty. This is effectively a mulligan, though not called so.

There are a number of stories claiming to tell of the origins of the mulligan, none of which can be verified.

I was recently told a story that emanates from the Royal Montreal Golf Club (incidentally, the oldest golf club in North America, founded 1873) about a Dr Mulligan. He lived across the lake from the club and used to row across to play golf. Because of this he was frequently puffed out when he arrived, so if his first shot was bad his partners would allow him to take a second. If anyone who plays at that club would like to verify that story, it would be appreciated.

On the other hand, a Mulligan may be named after a golfer who kept replaying shots. The USGA museum mentions a David Mulligan who played at St Lambert Country Club, Montreal. Whether he was the origin of the term or not is open to debate but the club is so certain of their ownership of the term that they have erected a plaque to commemorate it. However, the same authority names a John "Buddy" Mulligan of the Essex Falls Club, New Jersey, who was also known for replaying shots.

There is also the possibility that it is an ethnic slur aimed at Irish immigrants who took up the game in the north eastern states of the USA but weren't known as competent golfers.

A final version is that it originated in American saloons, where a free bottle of booze was placed on the bar for customers to dip into. This bottle was called a mulligan. As this was a "free shot" it got transferred to the golf course with the same meaning.

Historically, the mulligan appears to have entered golfing terminology sometime in the 1920s or 30s.

The opposite of a mulligan is a gilligan, when your opponent thinks your shot was too good and asks you to play it again. This would assume that it had been agreed that gilligans and/or mulligans had been agreed to be played before the round started.

N is For

Never up - never in

A term sometimes used by golfers when they fail to get close to the hole with a chip from beside the green or with their first putt. It means that it wasn't a reasonable shot as it had no chance of getting in the hole.

Just as a matter of fact, never in the history of golf has the hole moved towards the ball. If you want to sink a putt, you can't leave it short.

Nicknames

This entry doesn't refer to the nicknames given to people, but to nicknames given to golf shots.

Over the years, golfers have come up with a lot of different ways to describe a golf shot (usually a bad one). Many are offensive in one way or another, unfortunately, but a few can be included in this book. Some of these might not work if you aren't British, but you can always make up your own:

An Adolf Hitler – two shots but still in the bunker.
An Alistair Campbell – too much spin
A Chuck Berry – in the trees (no particular place to go)
A condom – safe, but didn't feel good.
A Cuban – needed another revolution (a putt that is a fraction short of the hole)
An Eva Braun – picked up in a bunker
A Gerry Adams – hitting a provisional
A Jeremy Corbyn – too far left
A Kate Moss – far too thin
A Nigel Farage – too far right.
A Rebecca Adlington – always in the water
A Saddam Hussein – going from bunker to bunker.

A son-in-law – not what you were hoping for.
A Tony Blair – fading right
A Vinnie Jones – a nasty kick when you least expect it.

And the latest addition to the genre: a Dominic Cummings – A long drive but with trouble at the end of it.

Nil return

Also sometimes called a non-return. It means failing to submit a scorecard for a competition either because the round wasn't completed or because the score was embarrassing and the golfer doesn't want anyone to see it.

A nil return is sometimes used as a ploy to prevent a handicap adjustment ahead of a competition, but this will be prevented in future under the World Handicapping System, as committees will be able to enter a "penalty score" for a golfer who nil returns.

The penalty score is always equal to the golfer's most recent best round and consequently nearly always results in a downward handicap adjustment.

Nineteenth Hole

A golfing term for the clubhouse bar. Not heard much these days.

O is For

Obstructions

An obstruction is usually an object that wasn't part of the golf course when it was designed and therefore shouldn't be allowed to interfere with the golfer's ball or swing when he takes his shot.

There are two types of obstruction recognised under the RoG and to differentiate between them it is usually necessary to refer to the local rules printed on the reverse of the scorecard for the course.

Moveable obstructions are objects which, as you might suspect, may be moved without penalty, to permit a golfer to take their shot. The obstruction may be impeding the forward motion of the ball, or it may be impeding the golfer's swing. Either way, it may be moved. Small signs used around the golf course, indicating walking routes or GUR, "repair pitch marks" signs, stakes supporting ropes used to cordon off GUR and similar would all be moveable obstructions.

Immovable obstructions are things the player can't move but may take relief from by moving their ball. Typical immoveable obstructions are huts provided for shelter, bench seats, litter bins (though they may also be moveable obstructions) and young trees.

You would think that things that look alike would be treated in the same way under the RoG. Not so, I'm afraid.

Out of bounds markers used within course boundaries are often white stakes, similar to the red or yellow stakes that are used to mark the perimeter of water hazards. Apart from the colour they are identical.

The red and yellow hazard markers are treated as moveable obstructions and may be moved if they are interfering with the shot. But an out of bounds marker is not a moveable obstruction and therefore may not be moved. The ball has to be played "as it lies".

I'm sure there's reason for this, but I'm blowed if I know what it is.

Anyway, knowing your obstructions and how to deal with them may save you a shot.

Immoveable obstruction?

Out of Bounds

Just like most sports, the game of golf has to be played within the boundaries defined for it. On most courses these are perimeter hedges, fences, walls and some natural features such as streams or rivers. The local rules on the reverse of the scorecard will detail the out of bounds for the course.

If the ball crosses the course boundaries then the golfer is "out of bounds", incurs a penalty shot and must take another shot from where they last played.

There are also "internal" out of bounds which are usually aimed at protecting property or people. Typically, a car park close to the edge of a golf course will be designated out of bounds, as will the practice putting green, driving range etc. Of course, making an area out of bounds doesn't stop a ball from being hit there, as many a golfer has discovered when getting back to the car park to find their windscreen smashed and a golf ball lying on the seat.

I have lost count of the number of times I have had to pull out of a shot while on the driving range because a golfer on the 10th hole has wandered onto the range looking for their ball. It's out of bounds - don't go looking for it!

Areas may also be put out of bounds in order to prevent people from spending a long time looking for their ball in dense undergrowth. It doesn't work, they will look anyway because golf balls cost money!

Elsewhere in this book I describe the situation at our club where a neighbouring fairway to the hole in play is out of bounds to prevent golfers taking a risky shot over the clubhouse roof.

If your ball is going anywhere near an out of bounds area, please always play a provisional ball (see *Provisional ball*). It will save you a lot of time having to trudge back two hundred yards to play again when you find your ball has actually sneaked out of bounds by two inches. If you are with someone who may be in danger of going out of bounds with their shot, gently suggest that they take a provisional ball. If they refuse, beat them gently around the head with a 9 iron until they agree. It's your time they will be wasting if they have to return and play the shot again.

Going out of bounds always incurs a penalty.

P is For

Par

This is the score that should be achieved for any hole and the concept was first used at Coventry Golf Club (see *Bogey*), although it was originally called by another name.

The term "par" originated in the Stock Exchange where a stock's price could vary above or below its normal, or par, range. It may derive from "parity".

The first known use of the term in relation to golf was in reference to Prestwick's (at that time) 12 hole course in 1870.

A golf writer by the name of A H Doleman asked two professionals, David Strath and James Anderson, what score should be expected during that year's "Open", which was being played at Prestwick. They said that they expected a score of 49 to be about right. Dolman then referred to 49 as being "par for the course".

Young Tom Morris, a well-known professional of the day so named to distinguish him from his father, subsequently won The Open with a score of 2 strokes "over par" for three rounds of 36 holes. His score would therefore have been (3 x 49) + 2 = 149.

The introduction of the term par in America came later, with the establishment of the Ladies Golfing Association in 1893 and the men's in 1894. Both started to develop handicapping systems that used "par" as its basis and those were in place by the turn of the century.

In 1911 the American Golf Association (Men) laid down standard distances for the pars for different lengths of hole. These were:

Up to 225 yards - Par 3 (now up to 250 yds)
225 to 425 yards - Par 4 (now 251 to 470 yds)
426 to 600 yards - Par 5 (now 471 to 690 yds)
Over 601 yards - Par 6 (now over 690 yds)

However much we may like to think otherwise, we amateurs very rarely "par" a course. It isn't impossible, especially for those with a lower handicap, but for the vast majority of us it is just a dream, a bit like that one where we are out on a date with Rihanna (or is that just me?).

Penalties

This is a stroke (or strokes) that is added to a score when a rule has been breached, when a second ball has to be played or when the ball has to be moved in order to make it playable, other than where the RoG allow relief to be taken, e.g. immovable obstructions.

Failing to apply the correct penalty can result in a golfer being DQ'd from a competition.

All the actual shots played have to be counted, as well as the penalty, which is something that sometimes gets overlooked.

Pitch marks

Something that too many golfers fail to repair when they make them.

When a ball lands on the green with force, especially when landing from height, it will often make a dent in the surface. This is called a pitch mark, because that is where the ball pitched. Pitch marks should always be repaired and golfers should carry a small tool, called a pitch mark repairer, in their pocket with which to repair them They are available in all pro shops and are quite cheap. Some courses even give them away for free in order to encourage their use.

Pitch marks not on the green can't be repaired. That's part of "playing the course as you find it".

If a pitch mark is found on the line of a putt it may be repaired, but it will still leave the surface damaged, which may affect the putt.

The experts on the subject say that if a pitch park is repaired promptly, it will be unnoticeable twenty four hours later. But if it is left unrepaired it will take a month to repair itself.

Some while ago, signs started to appear at golf clubs that said the following:

"The average number of pitch marks made on greens during a round of golf is 8 per golfer. Assuming 130 rounds of golf are played per day, that means your greens receive an average 1,040 impressions daily, 31,000 per month. That's 374,000 per year. Are you wondering how to make your putt under these conditions? Repair your pitch marks."

I have lost count of the number of pitch marks I repair on my way around my course. On one green alone this month I know I repaired six - that is on one day, not in the whole month.

Part of the problem is that if golfers don't immediately see their pitch mark, they don't go looking for it. Come on guys - you know it's there. Take your putt, sink the ball and then go looking for your pitch mark while your partners are holing out. Even if you don't find yours, you'll find someone else's and you can repair that instead.

There is a school of through that suggests that all golfers who fail to repair their pitch marks should be executed. I wouldn't go as far as that but I wouldn't object to them being horse whipped.

Partners

These have been mentioned many times so far in this book. A good partner is a friend for life. A bad one is a pain in the you know what. What's worse is that you may be the bad partner and not even realise it because we're all too polite to say.

Playing partners are friends for life.

Practice

Also covered under "Driving range", but practice is something that amateurs, especially those with high handicaps, never do enough of.

A long time ago a pro golfer played a chip from off the green and it went into hole. Someone in the crowd shouted "Lucky shot", to which the golfer replied "The more I practice, the luckier I get".

It was Arnold Palmer who is credited with the quote, though it may have started off during the Cuban revolution and have nothing to do with golf. But that doesn't matter, it is the message that is important. Good golfers are good golfers because they have a talent for the game, but they stay ahead of the pack because they practice. Even a poor golfer can improve if they practice.

Ask the average amateur when they last practiced and they will probably look at you as though you have mental health issues.

I know, I'm a hypocrite because I don't spend much time practicing. In fact the last time I was on a driving range was four months ago (around October 2019) and that was to see if my knee would hold up after surgery earlier in the year.

But there is a reason why "Practice makes perfect" became a popular saying and has been in use from at least the 1500s.

Prizes

As was established much earlier in the book, amateur golfers aren't allowed to compete for cash prizes, so they compete for non-cash prizes up to a value of £500. That is a quite a lot of money. I have never played in a competition that offered a prize that generous. But I suppose they do take place if they are sponsored events.

Most major prizes at our club come in at about £100. In 2018 I won a golf bag that was valued at that when I looked it up on the internet and I actually got £80 when I sold it through a well-known auction site.

That's one of the problems when you are playing in club competitions, the prizes will usually be golf related, which means that the golfer has probably already got one of whatever they win. Now, if your old one (whatever it is) is worn out and due for replacement, that's fine. But I had recently bought a brand-new golf bag of the same quality as the one I won. So I didn't have much use for my prize. It was great to win a prize, of course, but the proceeds of the sale went on a dinner for two with my wife. A voucher for that dinner would have been greatly appreciated and would have saved me a lot of time wrapping the golf bag in cardboard so I could post it to the buyer.

But getting golfing related prizes is so much easier for the committee. Give the pro shop a list of prizes to be awarded and a price range for each and let them see what they can come up with from their stock. Collect the prizes from the pro shop on the morning of the competition and arrange them on the prize table for the competitors to see what they might have won.

Minor prizes are usually gloves and golf balls. Both of those are appreciated because gloves wear out and golf balls get lost.

Pro

A person who wanders the golf club hinting to the members that their game might be improved by booking a lesson with him (or her).

No, I do them an injustice. They run the pro shop, which is an essential "front of house" for most golf clubs and they are the resident expert on all golfing related matters. Of course, amongst the services they offer are lessons and coaching and I have benefited from the odd lesson from time to time. I would probably benefit from some more but, like many amateurs, the idea of paying for something doesn't go down well.

There is a difference between a touring pro and a club pro. The touring pro may start as an amateur but have to turn professional because they have accepted a cash prize or simply to make money from the game. They gain their pro status by entering qualifying competitions. Most touring pros start their playing careers at junior level and graduate through the amateur hierarchy at club, county and national level, where they will have benefited from professional coaching.

Most touring professionals will have represented their country in amateur competitions before turning professional but that isn't a hard and fast rule. In the USA things are different. There, talented golfers can progress through college scholarship programmes, much as footballers and basketball players do. Tiger Woods came up that way, at Stanford University, where he studied economics between rounds of golf.

There are two routes to becoming a golf pro at a club. One is to study at a university that offers a recognised degree course. That is, recognised by the Professional Golfers' Association (PGA). This is a three year, full time course of study. As well as studying the game it also deals with the different aspects of golf club management.

To be accepted on the degree course, men need a handicap of 4.4 or less and women 6.4 or less. This provides credibility for the graduate, that they can actually play the game. They will also be expected to take part in golf tournaments while they are studying.

The second route is what might be described as "on the job training" or an apprenticeship. This is also a three year training course offered as "distance learning" while working at a golf club. Again, there is a handicap requirement.

Once qualified, professionals are encouraged to enter tournaments, again to provide some credibility to back up their status.

But back to what the pro is mainly known for, the provision of golf lessons. If you really want to improve your game, a visit to the club pro is probably the best way of doing it. The best pro's won't try to take your game apart, as that requires too much work to rebuild. They will merely correct the more glaring errors in you grip, stance etc and help to make fine adjustments.

Pro-Am

These are competitions that partner a professional golfer with an amateur. You could find yourself playing alongside one of the greats of golf.

Actually, you probably won't. The "am" part of many Pro-ams are usually "celebrities" because they attract the biggest crowds to the event. Pro-ams are often played on one of the practice days ahead of a tournament and are aimed at bringing spectators through the gates and into the tournament "village" where they can spend their money in the many shops and concession stands. However, they will raise money for charities at the same time.

Pro-ams are sometimes held as special fund raising events. In these sorts of events the "am" part of the partnership will have paid quite a lot for the privilege of playing, while the "pro" part will be giving their time for free in order to attract the "ams". It's how the charity makes its money. Spectators will also be allowed to buy tickets to see their heroes, both golfing and celebrity, to help boost the takings.

A more realistic event for the average amateur to play is the "am-am" event. Here one of the ams will be a celebrity (pop star, actor, comedian, sports star etc) who is also a keen golfer. The other am is the amateur who is prepared to pay to participate.

A friend of mine, very much a non-golfer, was once sent (under protest) to play in an am-am competition, because his company was one of the event sponsors and they needed someone there to represent the company on the golf course. His entry fee was paid by his employer.

He was partnered with a well know former cricketer who had been a national hero only a few years before and who was still instantly recognisable because of his commentating on TV and his charity work. Not only did my friend hack his way around the golf course, racking up a ridiculously bad score, but he had no idea who his playing partner was and when the subject of cricket was mentioned he voiced his opinion that it was a stupid game that went on too long (I can see his point).

Later, at the dinner that accompanied the event, the famous cricketer was called on as the guest of honour to make a speech, being given a fulsome introduction from the sponsor (who was also my friend's employer), who had turned up just for the meal. My friend made the excuse of going to the toilet and made a hasty escape. Happy ending: he kept his job and was never sent on that sort of thing again - which suited him.

Pro-shop

This is a place of great temptation. Expect to leave it very much the poorer than when you entered.

The pro shop is where you go to buy all the things you need in order to play the great game of golf. To be sure, you will be able to find cheaper prices in a well known high street store and on the internet, but that doesn't help you much when you turn up at the golf course to find that you left your golf shoes at home or that you're down to your last golf ball.

Once inside the pro shop you will find all sorts to tempt you into buying far more than you thought you ever needed. While I'm here, you may say, I may as well stock up on tee pegs. Oh, that shirt looks nice, I wonder if they have it in my size. A sale, did you say? 20% off. I'd better take a look then.

Is that the latest Ping driver there? The one they've been advertising on Sky Golf? I wonder what it feels like. I promise, I'll just hold it, I won't take it out on the range to try it out. Oh, a free bucket of practice balls you say. Well, it won't do any harm to give it a go I suppose. Yes, it does feel good and I'm pretty sure I was getting an additional ten yards compared to my old driver.

(That's it, you are doomed. As soon as you refer to a club as "my old ..." the sale is as good as made).

What's that, you'll knock ten percent off as I'm a member? Sounds like you've got yourself a deal.

Now, what was it I came in for? Oh yes, can I just book a tee-time for Sunday.

And that's how it seems to work.

But the pro shop isn't just about selling you loads of things you never even realised you needed. It is, as suggested above, where you go to book your tee-times, to book in before play, to book (and pay for) a buggy and so on and so forth.

For the visitor, the pro shop is their first point of contact with the club, both on the phone and in person. It is the club's shop window.

But it still an Aladdin's cave as well, so best to leave your credit card in the car before you go in. No, your car is just outside. Better to leave your credit card at home. Or better still, chop your credit card into little pieces.

A place of great temptation!

Provisional Ball

A provisional ball is something that amateurs should play far more often than they actually do. They save a lot of time.

Technically speaking a provisional ball is one that is played "just in case". Just in case you have gone out of bounds or just in case your ball has got lost in that thick area of undergrowth it was heading towards.

It is an immutable rule of golf that a shot played with a provisional ball is far superior to the original shot. This gives rise to the rather weak joke that "you should have played your provisional ball first."

I was thinking of having some balls made, marked with the words "provisional ball" just as a novelty. That idea is now copyright, by the way. I expect royalties if you use it.

If you play a provisional ball from the tee it is known as playing "three off the tee". That is the original shot, a penalty for playing the provisional ball and the shot that is actually played with the provisional ball. In some cases it has become five off the tee and even seven off the tee. There may be a world record for the highest number of "… off the tee" shots, but if there is I don't know how many it may be.

If your original ball has gone out of bounds or you decide your ball really is lost, then you play your provisional ball from wherever it is. If you find your ball and it isn't out of bounds, then you pick up your provisional ball and continue as though it never existed.

If your provisional ball didn't go as far as the original shot, you may continue to play it until you get to where you think your original might be before you have to decide which ball is the one in play or that decision is made for you by circumstances.

Playing a provisional ball is supposed to save you time, so you don't have to walk all the way back to where you started and play another ball. This is not an excuse for taking more than the allotted three minutes to look for your ball.

Putting

Putting should be the easiest shot in golf. You are playing on a relatively smooth surface, the ball doesn't have to go far and there is no risk of losing the ball or going out of bounds.

So why does it always seem so hard?

I have been on the green with two putts available to make par and have walked off with a bogey and even a double bogey. Why? How can that happen?

As with many things, practice is all. Most golf clubs provide a practice putting green for use before you step out onto the course. The grass should be of the same texture and the same length as that on the greens that you will play on later. This allows you to work out the "speed" of the greens before you have to play on the real thing. The best putting greens have contours and slopes similar to those you will play later, allowing you to "read" the lines that you have to take, thus "getting your eye in".

Most putting greens, like most driving ranges, are deserted, no matter how busy the golf course. Once again, amateurs don't spend nearly as much time practicing their putting as they should do.

Scratch golfers are reckoned to go around courses with an average of 31 putts, and the average golfer should be able to manage 35. Webb Simpson was the best putter on the USPGA tour in 2019 and he averaged slightly under 30 putts (1.665 putts per hole). Jordan Spieth managed an average 27.5 in 2015.

So why do so many amateurs average in the high 30s? Read the above again.

Then work out how you can reduce your handicap by a couple of strokes just by improving what should be the simplest part of the game.

But we're amateurs. We don't do that.

Putting is actually something you can practice at home, on your living room carpet. If you have a cat, it will even join in with the game. Don't try to putt on a wooden or tiled floor. And don't tell your spouse I suggested this.

Q is For

Quit or quitting

The opposite of killing the ball. You "quit on the shot" when you fail to commit fully and under-hit. Very common in putting if the golfer isn't convinced they have chosen the right line or the right distance.

Just like killing the ball, the failed shot also results in much cursing and swearing.

R is For

R & A

Originally it was the Royal and Ancient Golf Club of St Andrews, it became the spiritual home of golf and arbiter of the rules of golf as played in the UK and those countries that recognise its authority; which is quite a lot of countries.

The R&A is now a separate entity, hence the change of its name. It is now solely concerned with the governance of British golf, golf rules education and the management of certain golfing tournaments, but specifically The Open and the qualifying rounds for it.

The golf club itself is now known as St Andrews Links (see *St Andrews*).

Rake

You wouldn't think it necessary to have an entry for what amounts to a piece of gardening equipment, but given the state of some bunkers it is clear that some golfers don't know what a rake is or what it is used for. So, for their benefit, a rake is piece of gardening equipment used by golfers to smooth out the sand in bunkers after playing a shot in a bunker.

It is a universal rule that the rake is always positioned at the furthest point in the bunker in relation to the point from where the shot is to be played.

Ready golf

There used to be strict rules of etiquette with regard to which order golfers played their shots, not only on the tee, but also for subsequent shots on the hole. To go out of turn was disrespectful and could earn the errant golfer s sharp word of censure. I won't go into the nuances of this as it has now been confined to history.

Instead, golfers are now encouraged to play "ready golf", that means the golfer who is ready to play their shot is the golfer who plays next - providing it is safe to do so. This means that, in theory at least, the game is speeded up. You no longer have to wait while the golfer who scored lowest on the previous hole removes his jumper, marks his card, has a cup of coffee and eats a banana, before he takes his shot.

There is that caveat, however. It must be safe to do so. If there is a golfer in front of you that is in danger of being hit by your ball, then it is safer to wait for them to get out of the way. They don't even have to be directly in front to be in danger, as I have found out to my cost. In practice most golfers wait behind the one who is furthest from the hole to play their shot before walking forward to their ball, so that risk is reduced.

Does it speed things up? Not yet. Old habits die hard and it is still common for golfers to defer to the lower handicapper on the first tee and the lower scorer on the next etc. You can also get a bit of an advantage when it comes to putting, by waiting for the golfer furthest from the hole to putt first, so you can see how their ball runs - but you didn't hear that from me, right!

But the whole point of "ready golf" is to actually be ready when it is your turn to play. There is little more frustrating than being ready to move on, just to watch your partner only starting to prepare for the shot after you have played: Consulting the scorecard and course planner, checking their sat nav, throwing up grass to gauge the wind speed and direction, selecting their club, taking their stance, changing their mind and going back to select another club (repeat the last four steps as often as required). All that should have happened while you were taking your shot. There are now some golfers I won't partner thanks to this sort of behaviour.

In match play, the order in which players play is a fundamental of the game and if you go out of turn your opponent may ask you to play your shot again (without penalty), so the principle of ready golf doesn't apply. However, you may go out of turn if given permission by your opponent.

Relief

A word that has more than one meaning, but in golf it means to be allowed to move one's ball without incurring a penalty.

Typically, a golfer will get relief from GUR, abnormal ground conditions, temporary water (see *Water*) and immovable obstructions.

It can be very beneficial to one's score to know where you can take relief, especially under local rules.

There's more than one type of relief.

<u>Round (of golf)</u>

Surprisingly there is no set number of holes that must be played to constitute a "round" of golf. In social golf the players can agree this amongst themselves, perhaps choosing to play only 9 holes or maybe the 12 nearest holes to the club house etc.

    For competitive golf, the committee sets the number of holes that constitutes the round as part of the rules for the competition. Failing to complete the designated round is grounds for disqualification. It should be said, however, that most competitions are played over 18 holes, with occasional evening competitions played over 9 holes.

9 hole courses often have additional tees so that they can create 18 holes with different characteristics. In some cases the differences are minor, a slight change of angle or distance to the hole, but more creative designs include different hazards depending on which tee is being used.

Shiskine Golf and Tennis Club on the Isle of Arran is probably one of the last remaining courses to have anything other than a 9 or 18 hole layout. It isn't an old course, however. The earliest reference to the club is in a magazine article in 1897. It is built mainly on reclaimed land. The original course was only 9 holes and it was extended to 18 holes before World War I robbed it of 6 holes that were used for military purposes. After the war they were deemed unfit for purpose and abandoned. To make up 18 holes for competition purposes the 1st, 2nd, 9th, 11th and 18th holes are played a second time, along with a 15th hole that uses a different tee on the 4th hole.

Round (of drinks)

Thanks, I don't mind if I do. Pint of lager please.

Rough

As noted earlier in this book, there is no formal definition of rough in the RoG. Suffice to say it is anywhere that is not "close mown". This can cover a multitude of types of terrain, from grass that is just a bit longer than that of the fairway to deep jungle that it requires a machete to hack a way into.

In most cases rough just means deeper grass, but even then the depth can reach up to the knees. Getting out of such deep rough is fraught with problems. The grass tends to cling to the club head as it passes through, slowing it down, so even a good strike may only send the ball a few feet, while remaining within the area of rough. In the worst cases the ball might actually be driven only a few inches deeper into the roots of the grass itself.

Choosing which club to play in rough is often difficult. It is generally considered wise to sacrifice length for lift by using a "lofted" club (7, 8 or 9 iron or a pitching wedge) but I have seen people use a 3 wood, on some occasions more successfully than others. There is a saying, "He who takes wood in rough, has wood in head", but some people seem to get away with it.

Finding a ball in the rough is time consuming and is to blame for most slow play.

The only really good advice to be offered on the subject of rough is "don't go in it!", but of course that is far easier said than done. The other advice, in terms of course management, is if you are in thick rough, declare the ball "unplayable" and take relief under penalty. However, the thought of taking a penalty is enough to discourage most amateurs, which is why they then score a 10 on that hole.

And yes, I do mean me.

Rules of Golf (RoG)

The player's edition of the Rules of Golf (ROG) is pocket sized but runs to 160 pages of very small print. The player isn't supposed to know the entire contents off by heart but is supposed to know enough to know that there is a rule covering certain eventualities. The relevant rule can then be consulted using the book, so as to decide how to proceed under whatever circumstances have arisen.

Within those 160 pages are laid out twenty four actual rules, which are then subdivided into paragraphs, sub paragraphs and clauses, each of which describes a different circumstance.

And that is the player's edition. The full rules are much longer and more detailed.

I would like to offer my own version of the rules:

1. Once placed on the tee, the ball may not be touched again until it is lifted out of the hole.
2. If it becomes necessary to touch the ball, a penalty may or may not apply.
3. If you aren't sure if you have incurred a penalty, err on the side of caution and assume that there is a penalty, until you can find out for sure after you have completed the round.
4. The rules have changed since you started playing golf a hundred years ago, so what was a rule then may not be a rule now.

That last rule is specific to seniors' golf. On many an occasion I have been told that such-and-such applied, only to find out later that the rule was changed in 1921 or whenever.

There is an old saying in golf that covers most eventualities: "Play the ball as it lies; play the course as you find it; and if in doubt as to what to do, do what is fair."

The RoG are established in the UK by the R&A. They used to be the Royal And Ancient Golf Club of St Andrews, but are now a separate body in their own right, whose primary purpose is the governance of the game, rather than being a golf club. For this reason, the governing body for golf in the UK is now known by this shortened title.

While being a well-respected organisation throughout the world, the R&A's remit extends only as far as the shores of the UK and those other countries that choose to recognise it as their authority with regards to the game of golf. There is one other governing body for the sport in the world and that is the United States Golf Association (USGA).

As golf is an international game which has to be played under one set of rules (much like football or rugby), it means that it takes time to negotiate changes to the rules between the two governing bodies. For this reason, there is a revision cycle of four years duration. However, not every cycle results in a new release of the rule book.

Some result in only minor amendments. In specific circumstances an amendment may be made simply to meet a specific need.

An example of this was when ultra-high definition television came into being.

A golf ball is vulnerable to the same laws of physics as any other object and this can lead to tiny movements as vibrations act on the ball when it is otherwise static. These are so tiny that the player is probably unaware that the movement has happened. But when the ball is magnified up to two feet in diameter in ultra-high definition and slow motion, the movement becomes more apparent.

Tournament organisers and TV stations were inundated by e-mails and Tweets from armchair golfers who had spotted these slight movements, which resulted in some players suffering penalties because it was deemed that they caused the ball to move.

Professional golfers, by and large, are an honest lot and if they know that they have transgressed the rules they will own up, very often declaring the transgression themselves. However, they were becoming very disgruntled over being penalised for transgressions they didn't even know they had committed. Both the R&A and USGA saw their point of view and rushed out an amendment to the RoG that stated that unless the movement was visible to the naked eye, without electronic assistance, the ball was deemed not to have moved.

But the amateur doesn't have to worry just about the RoG, because there are also the Interpretations of the Rules of Golf (IRoG from here on) which is a separate and very hefty tome.

The IRoG is to golf what legal precedents are to the judiciary. If a tournament or club committee can't make a decision on the RoG based on the evidence available to them, they can refer the matter to the R&A or the USGA. Having made the rules, those bodies are best able to interpret the intentions of them, as well as the precise interpretation of the language used. As any lawyer can tell you, words and phrases can have more than one interpretation and individuals always favour the interpretation that benefits them. Hence the IRoG.

Once the R&A and/or the USGA have published their decision, it is binding and whatever it is, it must be used to decide all similar cases. But every year the R&A and USGA is asked to make yet more decisions, so the interpretation of the rules is far from being a settled matter.

Having said all that, in terms of day-to-day golf, most amateurs understand the rules well enough not to need to refer matters to the committee.

But when it comes to social golf, i.e., that not involving a competition organised by the committee, things can sometimes get a bit murky. Players, especially close friends, will often overlook a minor transgression, such as a ball being moved slightly if it doesn't present the offending player with a clear advantage. However, if one of the other players isn't granted such leniency later in the round, fights can break out. People who have been bosom buddies for years have been known to stop talking to each other for the rest of their lives.

In the worst of cases, players have been known to concede putts from great distances for their friends but argue over tiddling little six inchers for people they don't favour.

I am as guilty as anyone when it comes to these things, I guess, but it serves to remind me that the RoG are there for a reason. But sticking rigidly to the rules can sometimes seem a bit curmudgeonly and unsociable when all you are playing for is to decide who's going to pay for the tea at the end of the round.

S is For

Scores

The scoring in golf is based on how many shots were taken to complete the hole, which accumulate to provide a score for the entire round. So far, so simple. But golfers wouldn't be golfers if they couldn't make things more complicated.

So we invented new ways of scoring called stableford (see *Stableford*), medalford and match play. There may be others that I haven't come across as some clubs invented their own along the way and some of those may still be in use.

But in the end, the thing you have to do is count how many strokes you played, then add the number of penalties (if any) you incurred.

Score card

The thing on which you write your score. On the reverse you will usually find a précis of the Local Rules.

You would think that there would be nothing more to say about scorecards, wouldn't you? You would be wrong.

Some golfers of my acquaintance have been filling in scorecards for decades but still manage to get them wrong. For the most part that doesn't matter too much. So long as the committee can work out what you have scored they tend to accept it. But that doesn't mean the amateur has to make life harder for them.

All scorecards require the golfer to provide the same information:

- Name
- Date
- Competition name (there may be more than one competition running on the same day)
- Handicap

- Marker's name (it is normal to swap cards, so someone else is writing down your score while you write down theirs, making you the "marker" for their card)
- Marker's handicap
- Number of strokes the player claimed for each hole.
- The player's total score for the round.

The marker also writes their own score on the card they are scoring, so that they can keep track and do a cross check with the person marking their own card. This allows for mistakes to be identified and corrected.

That is literally it. You don't even have to convert strokes to stableford points because that is the committee's job. So why are so many scorecards such a mess?

I have already commented on the fact that many scorecards are submitted without being signed, which results in disqualification. You have to wonder at the fact that someone has looked at the box marked "signature" and said to themselves, "I wonder what goes in there?"

Scratch and scratch golfer

These are mythical beings who play golf with mermaids for partners, while riding unicorns.

To be serious, it just means a golfer who is so good that their handicap is zero. Their nett score is also their gross as they have nothing to deduct. Remarkably, a scratch golfer still won't be good enough to play on the pro tours, because to win there you must be able to score birdies, not just pars.

Secretary

The workhorse of the golf club and also probably the most influential person outside of the club management.

In most golf clubs, being club secretary is a voluntary post that requires the investment of several hours every week to keep on top of things. When changes to the rules or the handicapping system are introduced, someone actually has to understand them so they can be communicated to the club members. This role often falls to the Secretary because it is easier than trying to find someone else to take the role on.

As can be imagined, it isn't easy to find someone to take on the role of Secretary, so if you have a volunteer, cosset him (or her). You may never find another person willing to do the job.

If you see someone old and bent, staggering around the club looking worried and overtired, it is probably the Secretary.

Seniors

Anyone over the age of 55 can play as a senior, but in practice they tend to wait until retirement.

Most golf clubs have a seniors' section (they don't always call it that) which manages its own competitions and plays on weekdays - because they can.

The seniors' section at our club attracts fields of over forty for some of its summer competitions. That's more than some clubs get as entries for competitions held at weekends. Are we unique in this? Probably not but it is good to know that we have a well supported seniors' section.

The one problem with seniors' golf is that seniors have a lot of time on their hands, which means that they have plenty of time to argue over things that younger club members would consider to be not worth the time and effort.

So, how about a joke about golfing seniors?

Fred was in the golf club one day when he bumped into Charlie. "Hello, Charlie." Fred said. "We don't see you on the course much these days?"

"No." Said Charlie. "It's my eyesight. I can't see where the ball lands anymore."
"That's a shame. I know you love your golf. Tell you what," said Fred. "Why don't you play with Harry. He's got eyes like a hawk. Never loses a ball."
"OK, I'll do that." Says Charlie.
So, the next Wednesday, Charlie teams up with Harry and off they go. Charlie hits a pearl of shot and it flies over two hundred yards. Naturally, because of his eyesight, Charlie doesn't see where his ball lands. Charlie says to Harry "Did you see where that landed?" and Harry confirmed that he had. So Charlie sets off down the fairway, confidently following Harry. As they walk further and further, there is no sign of Harry locating the ball, so Charlie says "Have we reached my ball yet?"
To which Harry replies "What ball?"

Boom tish.

Shank

A shank is to a golfer what the iceberg was to the Titanic.

First, some technical detail to help make sense of the rest of the explanation.

The head of a golf club is attached to the shaft by a bit of the club referred to as the "hozel". The hozel is a short hollow cylinder forged or cast (welded on cheap clubs) into the club head, designed to accommodate the shaft of the club. The junction between the hozel and the shaft is the most common point at which clubs break as it is the weakest point in the club's design.

If the golfer strikes the ball with the hozel, rather than with the face of the club, the ball will fly off at unexpected angles, to the detriment of the golfer's game and score. This is known as a "shank".

Once an amateur has started to shank the ball, he or she is doomed. It seems to be almost impossible for amateurs to remedy the situation and they are destined to spend the rest of their life shanking their way around the golf course - or giving up the game entirely.

Not only will the individual amateur suffer, but all other golfers on the course will suffer, as shanking appears to be contagious. If you find yourself as the partner of a shanker, there is nothing to be achieved by remaining in their company. Save yourself! Get out while you can.

Naturally, a visit to the club pro for a lesson would probably provide a remedy for the shank, but as discussed under "Pro", amateurs never take lessons; they would rather suffer than pay for help.

Shape (of a shot)

There are basically three shapes that you can give a shot. There is straight, a draw or a fade. A draw moves the ball right to left as seen from the point of view of a right-handed player, while a fade moves the ball left to right.

All three of those shots require particulalr techniques and those techniques requite practice to learn them and make sure that they can be produced on demand.

It is therefore unsurprising that the amateur golfer can forget all three of those. For the amateur there is only the hook (right to left) or the slice (left to right). Doing anything else is just pure, blind luck.

Should've

My suggestion for an alternative name for golf, as in "I should've taken an 8 iron" or "that putt should've gone in!"

This morning I told my wife I was off for a game of "should've" and she laughed. I think it might catch on.

Slope system

The USGA has operated a slope system in the USA for some time now, but it is a new thing for British golf.

Basically the slope system recognises that not all golf courses have been created equal, so when a golfer plays another course, especially in a competition, they may gain an advantage or suffer a disadvantage because their handicap is based on the difficulty of their home course.

For example, the club where I am a member is recognised as being relatively easy in golfing terms. It has several short par 4 holes and one short par 5. While the addition of hazards has increased the difficulty over the years, it will never be the same challenge as some other courses. It is only par 70 and has an SSS (see *Standard scratch*) of just 67.

So, when golfers from our club play against one of our near neighbours, a par 72 course with a length five hundred yards greater and an SSS of 70, our golfers struggle to compete on equal terms. In golfing parlance, our handicaps don't travel well.

The slope system seeks to compensate for this. It allows a golfer to add or deduct strokes from their handicap, depending on where they are playing.

The introduction of the slope system into the UK is set to coincide with the introduction of the World Handicap System (WHS) which seeks to standardise the various methods used to calculate handicaps around the world. It is due to launch in November 2020.

Slope ratings start at 55 and go up to 155 with an average of 113. When players visit courses with slope ratings above that of their home course they will be allowed to add strokes to their handicap and below that they will have to deduct strokes.

At the time of writing, I am still waiting for information on how to calculate handicaps using the slope system, or how this will be interpreted for "match play" competitions against our neighbours. At the moment it remains under the heading of "dark arts".

Slow Play

This is the bane of golf. It creates more clubhouse discussion than any other golfing topic (even more than handicaps) and more committee discussions as well.

The R&A recognises slow play as an evil and the 2019 version of the RoG changed some rules in the hope of speeding things up. Rule 1 of the RoG, the very first rule in the book, refers to golfers playing at a "prompt pace" as part of the standards of player conduct expected on the golf course. Unfortunately, they don't define what "prompt pace" actually means, leaving it open to individual interpretation. The R&A does, however, produce a "pace of play" manual and some helpful videos on the subject, which can be found on their website (see *Sources*, at the end of the book).

A useful fact gleaned from the R&A's website is that if each golfer takes just 5 seconds less over each shot, the duration of the round can be shortened by 25 minutes.

Even professional golfers aren't immune to slow play. On one golfing website, in 2019, the Top 5 slowest players are named as (in ascending order of slowness): Jordan Speath, Jason Day, Ben Crane, Bryson DeChambeau and J B Holmes. But this is not a new problem. In the past Nick Faldo, Bernhard Langer and Tiger Woods have all made it into that Hall of Shame and several professionals have been penalised for slow play.

Why would I bother to name the top 5 slow pros in a book about amateur golf? Because, just as with bunkers not being raked, that's where I think the problem starts.

Amateurs spend a lot of time watching pro golf on TV and they then seek to emulate the pros when they play their own games. After all, if the pros play that way, that must be the way to play, mustn't it?

If a pro takes several practice shots, so must the amateur. If the pro spends a long time eyeing up the shot, consulting their course notes and chatting to their caddy, so must the amateur. In the amateur's case it will be chatting to their partners because they don't have a caddy, but you get the idea. And if the pro saunters along the fairway as though they have all the time in the world, so must the amateur.

What the amateur forgets is that there is a fifteen minute gap between the tee-times (see Tee-time) for each group on the pro circuit. Golf clubs don't have that luxury. To make money they have to get as many golfers through the course in a day as is possible, which means tee-times that are only ten minutes, or even eight minutes, apart. This means that it is far easier for games to get backed up behind each other if one group is playing slowly by emulating their heroes on the pro tour.

But it's like the slow driver on the country road that never looks in their rear-view mirror. All they ever see is an open road in front of them, uncluttered by other traffic. They don't see the fifty-car tailback they have created with their slow driving. Exactly the same applies to the slow groups on the golf course. Unless they look back over their shoulders, all they will ever see is a clear fairway and an empty green. They won't see the two, or even three, groups on the previous tee fuming at having to wait, yet again, to play their tee shots.

It is a sad fact of life that as we get older we start to slow down. That would make you think that older golfers are the worst culprits when it comes to slow play. It is actually the opposite. It is younger players that seek to emulate the pros more, so it is the younger players that tend to be the slowest. This isn't a hard and fast rule, of course, but it certainly seems that if I am following a slow group they will all be under fifty and often under thirty. Just sayin'.

There are several factors that affect pace of play, other than just the behaviour of the golfers. There is the actual management of play - what golf clubs do to improve the pace of play - and also the course design and set-up. For example, keeping the rough between the front of the tee and the start of the fairway to a minimum (what is known as "mandatory carry") so that most golfers have a fighting chance of clearing it with their tee shot. As landing in that rough is likely to stop the ball dead, it will not only be necessary to stop and look for the ball, but also to play an additional shot to get out of the rough.

We all know slow players and some golfers refuse to play alongside them, but it doesn't make any real difference, because the slow player is out there somewhere, even if they are five groups ahead on the course and therefore out of sight. If you are waiting on a tee or in the middle of the fairway it is because, somewhere up ahead, someone isn't being courteous and keeping the game moving at a "prompt pace."

But finding out who it is and penalising them (which is a permitted sanction) is another matter.

So, other than the difficulties in identifying the culprits, why don't golf clubs penalise members for slow play? I can only conclude that it is a commercial consideration. Penalising golfers could result in them throwing their toys out of the pram and leaving the club to go elsewhere. That loses the club not only their membership fee, but the money they spend in the bar.

But failing to penalise people means the problem will persist as there is no reason for it to end, so we can expect slow play to continue to be a hot topic for many a year.

Please - just make sure it isn't you that's the culprit.

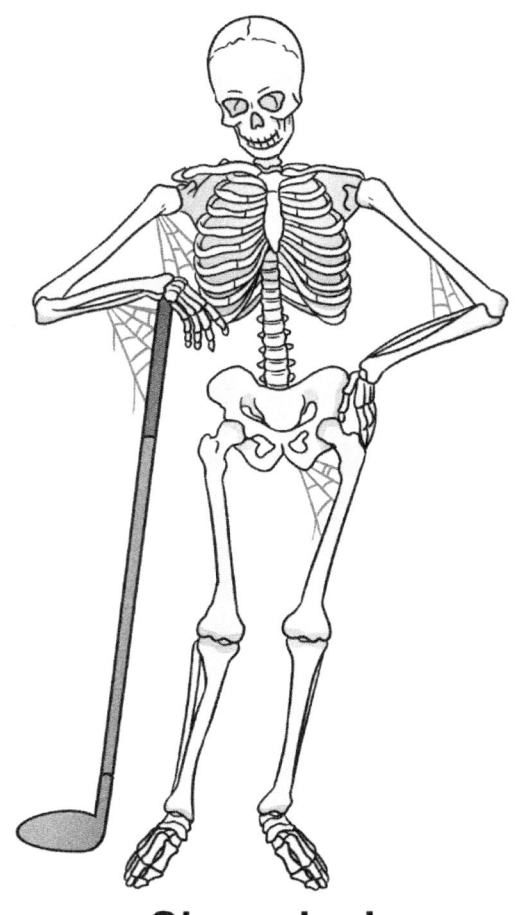

Slow play!

Smoking

You are permitted to smoke on a golf course. if you are golfing with me, I'd rather you didn't (unless standing downwind, but there's no actual rule preventing you).

Social golf

Any game of golf that isn't part of an organised competition. Unless a golfer is playing by themselves, in which case it is anti-social golf.

Societies

Societies are the pirates of golf. They swoop down, pillage the course then disappear back over the horizon.

That is the way that societies are seen by many amateurs who are members of golf clubs. I would like to challenge that view. But, first of all, what is a golf society?

A golf society is any group of golfers who get together to play the game on a casual basis, but who have no regular club of their own. They may be a formally structured group with their own captain and committee, or they may be a more ad hoc set-up. Some golfers are members of golf clubs, but also play in a society with their friends from work or their neighbourhood who aren't members of a golf club, or who are members at different clubs.

Golf societies can be made up from any group of people. Some professions and/or occupations have their own golf society. I am eligible to join both the RAF Golf Society and the Civil Service Golf Society. Some companies have their own golf society, though this is less common these days as businesses don't get so involved in the leisure time activities of their employees as much as they once did. There are societies based around social clubs, pubs and communities.

For many years I was a member of a golf society based around our village, though by the time I joined few of its members actually lived in the village anymore. But it is because of this involvement that I would like to challenge the perception of golf societies as a whole.

Perhaps the very presence of a golf society on a course is the start of this poor perception. If you are a member of a golf club and you turn up to play a casual eighteen holes with friends and you arrive to find forty members of a golf society standing beside the first tee, you are not going to be best pleased. But this is why a golf club has both a telephone and a booking system for tee-times. I have no sympathy if you didn't bother to book your tee time - because the society has had their tee times booked for weeks, if not months.

The second perception is that societies ruin courses because they don't take care of the course, e.g. they don't replace divots, rake bunkers or repair pitch marks. Perhaps I should quote from the Bible at this point, and specifically Matthew 7:5 "First cast out the beam from thine own eye; and then shalt thou see clearly to cast out the mote from thy brother's eye."

I have to say that club members are as guilty of these offences as anyone. This is evidenced most during the winter when there are no golf societies visiting, but I seem to spend half my round of golf repairing the pitch marks left behind by club members. During medal competitions, the footmarks left in bunkers by previous competitors make a difficult hazard more difficult and only members can enter medal competitions.

In many years of playing golf with a society I found that they were just as disciplined at looking after the course as the members at my own club. In some cases they were better. The more experienced golfers in the society always encouraged the beginners to take care of the course. The first I ever knew about repairing pitch marks and raking bunkers, I learned playing in a society, not at a club.

OK, not all societies are as good as others, but the majority do know how to play the game and how to take care of a golf course. After all, societies tend to play the same courses in rotation, so they probably want to be allowed back the next year. Having a bad reputation is bad for the society.

Societies are slow. This is probably the most justifiable objection, but it doesn't apply to all societies. Societies are often the place where new golfers learn the game. New golfers take far more strokes than experienced golfers and spend more time looking for lost balls etc. In our society some members were regular complainers about slow play from the society's own membership, so they aren't unaware of the problem. But, as every club member knows, slow play isn't confined to societies. It is a regular topic of discussion at the committee meetings of the club where I play. As a senior, we are usually the first people out on the course on a Wednesday, so we can't blame our five-and-a-half-hour round on anyone other than our own members.

Club members often don't consider the upside of societies. Firstly, it is the income from their visits that help to keep the club's own membership fees down. In many cases it is all that is keeping some golf clubs in business. A summer visit from a society of twenty golfers could be worth £700 in green fees alone. Then there are beer and food sales on top.

Like it or not, a visit from a golf society is helping to keep your club alive.

But, just as importantly, to keep the game of golf itself alive it needs new participants and one of the ways to get new golfers is through societies. It is the way I took up the game. The reputation of golf as a snobby game, played by people with posh accents and loads of money, makes it intimidating for a lot of people to take it up. This reputation is no longer justified in the case of the majority of golf clubs, but give a dog a bad name, as they say.

So, joining a society where you can learn to play golf with your mates is an attractive option for many people. When they discover that golf is no longer the snobby game it once was, they may even join a club - your club. But they won't do that if they aren't made to feel welcome when they visit with their society.

Lecture over; please now read on.

Societies are the pirates of golf.

Speed (of the green)

If your club ever measures the speed of its greens, then you are a very lucky golfer.

The speed of the green is the speed at which the ball will run which, in turn, governs the distance the putt will reach. Knowing the speed of the green can save a golfer putts, as it should prevent the putt from coming up short or racing past the hole.

The speed of a green is affected by the time of day (usually slower in the morning when the dew is still on the ground), the weather (wet greens are slower than dry ones) and the length of the grass (a freshly cut green will be faster than one cut the day before). Time spent on the practice green (never wasted anyway) can help to assess the speed of the green.

The speed of the green is measured using a stimpmeter (see *Stimpmeter*).

Standard Scratch

Standard scratch is something that shouldn't really bother the amateur, but for some reason is another regular topic of conversation during after-match chat in the bar. Perhaps it is because the whole system seems to be some sort of dark art.

The term refers to how the course actually plays in relation to par for the course. Imagine a scratch golfer going around your course, how many strokes could he expect to play? Would it be the 72 that it says on the scorecard, or would it be something different?

There are two types of standard scratch. The first is the standard scratch score (SSS). This is the score expected of our putative scratch golfer under average playing conditions. While the scorecard may show the course as being par 72, it may include short par 4s or par 5s where the scratch golfer could be expected to make a birdie. Or it could include some very demanding holes where even a scratch golfer might struggle to score a par.

SSS is assessed by measuring the course and through adjudication by golfers from the local county committee, using their golfing knowledge and experience. Most golf courses in the UK have just gone through* a major re-evaluation of their SSS in preparation for the introduction of the "slope system", discussed earlier.

So, the SSS is a more or less fixed entity. It is subject to review, especially when holes undergo major changes, such as the insertion or removal of hazards or the construction of new teeing areas (see *Tee-ing area*) to make a hole longer or (very rarely) shorter.

The second type of standard scratch is a much more moveable feast. It is adjusted in light of the performance of golfers during a competition and the playing conditions for the day. This means that the golfer's handicap won't necessarily be adjusted if the playing conditions are particularly benevolent or adverse.

As may be expected, golfers are likely to play better in good weather than bad and the course will be easier to score on when the weather is calm rather than when it is windy. It is noticeable that average scores are seasonal in nature, with better scoring in summer than in winter.

The scores of all the entrants to the competition are subjected to a complicated formula based on percentages of players in each handicap division and a competition standard scratch (CSS) is derived. This is used to adjust players handicaps based on the performance of the field as a whole. The introduction of computers into clubhouses has removed the burden of the calculation of CSS from the shoulders of the committee. The computer can do it quickly and accurately.

A "buffer zone" is established for the CSS, within which a player's handicap won't be adjusted. A category 1 golfer (handicap of 5 or less) has a buffer zone of + 1 stroke; for a category 6 golfer (handicap above 36) the buffer zone is + 6 strokes.

A player who achieves a score exactly matching CSS will not have their handicap adjusted; nor will a player whose score lies within the buffer zone. Only players whose scoring is better than the buffer zone will have their handicap adjusted.

So why is SSS and CSS such a talking point? Who knows? Maybe we amateurs just need something to talk about.

* Carried out in 2019.

Stableford

A system of scoring that assigns points for each hole played.

This scoring system was developed by Dr Barney Stableford, a golfer at the Glamorganshire Golf Club in Penarth, Wales in 1898 and its first known use in a formal competition was at Wallasey Golf Club in Cheshire in 1932.

The idea is that by assigning points for each hole, rather than keeping a running total of strokes taken, a golfer can have one or two bad holes and still return a competitive score. I have proved this to be true, as I have won stableford competitions even though I went into double figures on one (or more) of the holes in terms of strokes taken.

For each hole, two points are awarded for scoring a par. One point is awarded for a bogey and anything higher doesn't score at all. 3 points are awarded for a birdie, 4 for an eagle and for that rarest of birds, an albatross, you would get 5 points. The winner of the competition is the golfer with the highest number of points scored over the round.

The golfers' handicap is taken into account when working out their stableford points and how this is done is explained further under *"Stroke Index"*.

This format of scoring is also supposed to speed up play. Once you can no longer score on a hole there is no longer a reason to keep playing it, so you can pick up your ball and move to the next hole. In practice this doesn't seem to happen much and it is common for players to complete the hole anyway, unless they lose their ball along the way.

Most social games of golf are played using stableford scoring rather than "stroke play" (see *Stroke play*).

St Andrews

In the county of Fife (sometimes called the Kingdom of Fife) in Scotland, on the southern shores of the Firth of Tay, lies a small town (population 16,800 approx). Compared to other Scottish towns of a similar size it is unremarkable but for two things. The first thing of note about the town is that it is home to the oldest university in Scotland (founded 1413).

The second thing of note about the town is that it is the spiritual home of golf. The two things may well be related, because students at the university certainly rank amongst the first known golfers.

St Andrews Links, as it is now known, may not be where the game started, but it is where its rules were enshrined and its formal history as a game began.

In 1457 King James II (nicknamed Fiery Face with good reason) banned the playing of games (mainly football and golf) in Scotland. At that time games were considered a "public nuisance" because they were played in places that got in the way of other people. They were also described as "unprofitable". Whether they were unprofitable because no one knew how to make money out of them, or because the people who were playing them should have been finding a more profitable way of spending their time, isn't clear.

But the worst offence was probably that people were playing games on Sunday, the Sabbath day.

In 1522, King James IV, the grandson of James II, effectively repealed the law by buying a set of golf clubs in Perth. He is also recorded having spent money on golf equipment in 1504 at Falkland Palace, which was close to St Andrews and it is known that he played golf with the Earl of Bothwell. It is thought that St Andrews was the venue for their game.

A graduate of St Andrews university, Sir Gilbert Hay, is thought to be the first person to use the word "golf" in writing, in a poem written in 1460.

St Andrews adopted the rules of golf that had been written in 1744 by the Gentlemen Golfers of Edinburgh, referred to earlier. However, by that time it is known that at least fourteen other Scottish and English golf clubs had their own sets of rules. Later, The Royal and Ancient Golf Club, as it had become known, started selling subsidised printed copies of their rules and in 1897 they were given control of the rules with the assent of all the other British clubs in existence.

In 1873 The Open was played at St Andrews for the first time, though the competition had been in existence since 1860. When St Andrews is referred by commentators to as the home of The Open, they are inaccurate. That title rightly belongs to Prestwick, where it was first played and continued to be played until 1870. It was played at Musselburgh (now known as Muirfield) before St Andrews became part of a three course rotation. In 1920 St Andrews became solely responsible for the organisation of The Open and its qualifying competitions. Not that St Andrews was in any way "pushy", you understand.

Since those early days, St Andrews has grown and prospered as a club. They now boast 7 courses of various lengths and difficulties, of which the "Old Course", the original, is the jewel in the crown.

Unlike Augusta, visitors are able to play on this hallowed ground. As a matter of tradition, booking for the Old Course is by a public ballot which is held two days before the desired date of play. The other courses can be booked directly in the more usual manner. Green fees for the Old Course (correct at the time of writing) are £95 for the low season and £195 for the high season (20th Apr - 19th Oct).

I have yet to play golf at St Andrews, but it remains an ambition, (should any family members be reading this and wondering what to buy me for Christmas).

Stimpmeter.

Golf commentators on TV mention stimpmeters and stimp ratings quite a lot. It's the device used to measure the speed of a green.

A stimpmeter is actually quite a primitive tool. It consists of a metal trough about three feet long onto which a ball is laid. The end of the trough is raised up until the ball starts to roll downhill. The ball rolls off the bottom of the trough, which is resting on the green. The distance the ball travels across the green is then measured. The measurement is taken in two directions across the green (forwards and backwards), the two measurements are added together and then divided by two. This gives the stimp rating for the green.

More modern versions of the stimpmeter actually mount the trough on a frame at a fixed height, making it look like a miniature version of a slide in a children's playground, but both versions measure to about the same level of accuracy.

The higher the stimp rating, the faster the green.

Stroke

What overweight golfers have. This can also be caused by seeing the price of a gin and tonic in the clubhouse bar.

Also the act of striking a ball with the club. It consists of three parts: The back swing, the point of contact and the follow-through.

Sounds easy, doesn't it? Just wait until you try it for real.

Incidentally, it used to be the rule that no stroke had been played if the golfer didn't take a back swing, so just touching the ball with the club didn't count as a stroke. It is quite common for the amateur to nudge the ball off of a tee peg while setting up for their shot, at which point some wag will say "One".

Now the rule has been modified to include touching the ball while taking a practice swing. The golfer can "pull out" of his stroke at any time before the club strikes the ball, without it counting as a shot.

Now for a joke in poor taste.

A golfer returned home to be greeted by his wife. "My dear, you're so late. What happened?"

Golfer: It was poor Harry. He had a stroke on the 10th fairway."

Wife: "Oh, how tragic. But surely it couldn't have taken three hours to get help."

Golfer: "Well, it did. You have no idea how much time it takes having to play shot then drag Harry. Play a shot, then drag Harry."

Stroke Index

There are three sets of numbers that are always printed on a scorecard. There is the hole number, 1 to 18 in order of play (sometimes shown as two sets numbered 1 to 9, as at my club).

There is the par for each hole and then there is the stroke index. There may be a fourth set, which is the Stroke Index for the ladies, usually shown in a different colour of ink, which may be different to that of the men.

The stroke index (SI) for a hole is its difficulty rating, from 1 to 18. In the USA this is referred to as its "handicap" rating. An SI of one is assigned to the most difficult hole on the course and an SI of eighteen is assigned to the easiest hole. The "front 9" is assigned odd numbered stroke indices and the "back 9" is assigned the even numbers. However, this is more of a convention than a hard and fast rule. On our course only two holes of the front 9 have odd numbered SIs and on the back 9 only two have even numbers (what rebels we are!).

So, what is an SI for?

Basically, it tells golfers where they get their extra strokes when playing either match play or stableford formats. I have a handicap of 23, which means I am permitted to take an extra shot on every hole (a bogey) and still record 2 points for a par under the stableford scoring system. Deducting 18 from 23 leaves five shots of my handicap unaccounted for so I will get those on the five most difficult holes, (SIs 1 to 5 inclusive) and on those I will be able to make a double bogey and still count it as a par. With handicaps now going as high as 54, it means some golfers can score a triple bogey on every hole and still score them as pars under the stableford system.

Similarly, a golfer with a handicap of 15 will be able to score a bogey on holes with an SI of 1 to 15, but not on the holes with an SI of 16, 17 and 18 as those are the three easiest holes. On those three holes only a genuine par will be awarded 2 points.

In match play the handicap of the lower handicap golfer is deducted from that of the higher handicap golfer to establish how many strokes the high handicapper is "given". The SI tells the golfers where the high handicap golfer gets those shots. If I am playing a golfer with a handicap of 18, he will "give" me five shots. I will get one of those shots on each of the holes with an SI of 1 to 5, meaning that I can score a bogey on those holes and still "halve" it if my opponent scores a par. If we both score pars, I will win the hole.

SIs are not fixed permanently. They are subject to review based on the scores that are recorded in competitions and can also be reviewed when major changes are made to the golf course. In the twenty some years I have been playing at my course the SIs have been changed at least twice for some of the holes. As it costs money to reprint scorecards, any changes to the SI of holes is usually delayed until the old stock of scorecards has been used up and new stock is ordered.

Stroke play

The traditional form of scoring for golf, where each stroke is counted, plus any penalties incurred and the golfer achieving the lowest score is the winner. Handicaps are taken into account by deducting them from the gross score to record the nett score.

Stroke play is the normal scoring system adopted for the major competitions at clubs and also for the "monthly medal". For this reason stroke play is sometimes referred to as "medal play".

Swearing

With a game that relies so much on personal skill, the bounce of a ball and the random affects of wind and rain, trees and pinecones, there tends to be quite a lot of swearing on a golf course.

When I was Seniors Captain it got so bad I had to discuss the matter with the Lady Captain. She said that if the men didn't like it they should play at a different time.

Swing

A piece of child's play equipment, the hobby of certain consenting adults in involving a bowl and their car keys, or the motion of drawing back a golf club and using it to strike the ball.

T is For

Tees

A tee, or tee-peg, is used to raise the ball up off the ground. It makes for an easier shot and usually results in the golfer hitting the ball an increased distance. They may only be used for the initial shot on each hole (plus any "reloads" resulting from going out of bounds or losing the ball from the tee shot).

The use of tees wasn't always permitted in the game of golf. In the earliest of days golfers used to have to hit all of their shots off the ground. Later they were allowed to make a small heap of sand or soil to raise the ball. Finally the introduction of artificial tees was permitted.

The tee peg as we know it was first patented by William Bloxsom and Arthur Douglas, two Scotsmen, in 1889. The first commercially available tee peg was patented by Englishman Percy Ellis in 1892. In the USA the creation of the tee is credited to Dr George Franklin Grant in 1899. He was a dentist, so the stereotype of dentists playing a lot of golf is a well-established one.

The etymology of the word "tee" is from Scottish Gaelic, *Taigh*. This was a term used for the circular target area in the Scottish sport of curling. Fans of late night Winter Olympics coverage may be familiar with this sport; it's the only time anyone other than its participants ever take an interest in it.

This makes sense, because the original tees were a one yard area around the hole that had just been completed, from which the golfer started the next hole.

The introduction of the tee peg is thought to be the last major change in the rules of golf. Everything since is just an amendment or modification to existing rules.

Nowadays tees come in all shapes and sizes. Someone is always trying to reinvent them in the hope of making money out of golfers. But they fall into two major categories, wooden and plastic. Many golfers prefer to use plastic because they last longer. I prefer to use wooden tees because they are biodegradable.

For winter use there are even tees that don't have to be pushed into the ground. These look like rubber cones with the pointed end cut off to create a flat surface on which to support the ball. Generally they come in three different heights.

As with golf balls, a golfer will invest an inordinate amount of time in searching for a tee-peg that has gone astray (another cause of slow play). That's another reason for using wooden tees. If it isn't sticking out of the ground, then it will have been broken when the golf club hit it.

It isn't just winter that can cause difficulties getting a tee into the ground. In summer the hardness of the ground also makes it very difficult. On one occasion I suggested, jokingly, to my playing partners that I should carry a hammer around with me to hammer the peg in. One playing partner said he already did. I thought he was joking, but on the next hole he produced a small hammer from his golf bag and proceeded to demonstrate.

Teeing area

The area from which the golfer must play their tee-shot, the first shot on any hole. As described above, at one time this was a small area around the previous hole but has now developed into one of the five defined areas of a golf course.

According to the definitions of the rules of golf:

The *teeing area* is a rectangle that is two club-lengths deep where:

- The front edge is defined by the line between the forward-most points of two tee-markers set by the Committee, and
- The side edges are defined by the lines back from the outside points of the tee-markers.

Typically there are three teeing areas on each hole. The tee markers for these are colour coded so that you know which you should be using. In the UK the colours are red for the ladies, yellow for the men's tees in everyday use and white for the competition tees. Some courses also have blue tees for "championship" competitions and organised tournaments. I also know a course where one hole has black tees for use by golfers over 70 playing social golf, because that hole is so long an older golfer hasn't a hope of making par if playing off the regular tees.

The different coloured teeing areas may be in different locations on the hole. But each location must conform to the definition shown above.

If you look around and see that the ladies tees are behind you, you are probably facing in the wrong direction as they should be in front of you. While this is a good general rule, it isn't an absolute. Ladies play some long par 4s as par 5s and they may have the tee moved further back for that reason.

It is interesting to note that the old definition of a teeing area included the requirement that it be a level piece of ground, but the new definition doesn't. Having played on tees that had a domed surface or a slight slope, I wonder if this was a pragmatic decision.

Tee-time

An imaginary time when one or more golfers may be ready to play golf, but their partners will not be.

On any Sunday morning there will be three golfers standing on the first tee, holding everyone else up because their fourth partner is "running a bit late, but he'll be here any minute so just hang on a mo".

Eventually the fourth partner does turn up, but it takes him another five minutes to get his shoes on and unpack his equipment from his car, by which time there are probably a dozen golfers now waiting to tee off and getting very angry indeed.

As can be seen from the above description, for some golfers a tee-time can be a very flexible thing, depending on who is playing.

Rule 5.3a of golf stipulates that "You must start at (and not before or after) your starting time". You can be DQd for being more than 5 minutes early or late and you can suffer a penalty stroke for being less than 5 minutes early or late.

Only you won't. These penalties are rarely enforced, because there is no one around to enforce them. But as a rule of golf it is just as binding as any other. No rule of golf may be ignored by a golfer, so no golfer should ever tee off late (or early). In particular the rule is ignored frequently for social golf.

Golf clubs provide booking systems for tee-times so that golfers know when to arrive for their game. Technically speaking you shouldn't arrive to play golf if you haven't booked a tee time, whether it be on the sign-up sheet for a competition or on the Pro-shop's computer system. However, on a quiet day this isn't usually a problem and you will be allowed to slot yourself in where there is a gap in the bookings. But on a busy day you can't just rock up and hope to get a place on the tee.

But if you are booked to play at 10 a.m. and you're delaying your tee off to accommodate a late arrival, don't be surprised if you are verbally abused by other golfers.

The Open

This is the oldest open (in other words anyone can enter) tournament in golf and has been in existence since 1860. It was played at Prestwick from 1860 to 1870, moved to Musselburgh (Muirfield) for two years and then to St Andrews as part of a three course rotation.

Now the competition is rotated round nine courses, of which four are in Scotland. In 2019 Royal Portrush in Northern Ireland was included out of deference to Rory McIlroy.

Being an "open" competition, you too could play in The Open, at least theoretically. To do so you have to play through a series of qualifying competitions. The only amateurs guaranteed a place are the British amateur champion, his American and Asian counterparts and the winner of the Mark H McCormack medal. Since 2007 this prize has been presented by St Andrews to the amateur who leads the world amateur rankings.

Americans first played in The Open in 1921 when eleven golfers travelled across the Atlantic after receiving sponsorship from a fund set up specially for the purpose. One of those eleven, Jock Hutchinson, a naturalised American citizen, won the coveted claret jug in St Andrews, the town of his birth.

Golf clubs take great pride in former members qualifying for The Open whether it be as amateurs or professionals. The small Northamptonshire club where I play my golf has achieved that pinnacle twice. Sadly our hero hasn't yet made "the cut" to stay on for the weekend.

By tradition, The Open is always played on a links course.

Through the Green

Nobody ever knew what this meant. In the 2019 edition of the Rules of Golf the term was replaced by "general area". This is equally as obscure.

Tiger line

Nowadays this is often thought to refer to Tiger Woods, but its origins are much, much earlier, almost certainly in the 19th century. I am of an age where I remember hearing the term spoken long before Earl Woods said to Kultida Woods "Do you fancy an early night, Dearest?"

There was a golf club in India that marked its "out of bounds" areas with a series of painted metal tiger's heads mounted on posts, (possibly as a reminder that there might be tigers hiding in the long grass). On one particular dog leg hole, the best line to take with one's drive was straight along the line of tiger's heads. However, because of the risk of the ball straying out of bounds, this was also the most risky line to take, so it became known as "taking the tiger line".

As Michael Caine might say "Not a lot of people know that!"

Trees

Like everything else on a golf course, trees have the ability to ruin a perfectly good round of golf. I play on a course where there are quite a lot of trees, we even have one right smack bang in the middle of a fairway, so I know a little bit about this.

There are two problems with trees: where they are and what they are made of.

Every golfer will tell you the old adage about trees: they are 80% air. Statistically speaking this is true. There is a lot more air within that leafy shape than there is wood and leaves. But you can say the same about chicken wire; but you just try getting a golf ball through one of those little holes and you'll understand what I mean. A tree may be 80% air, but the bit you hit is always 100% wood.

On most golf courses the trees are arranged to flank the fairway, so a ball a little bit off line is liable to sneak in behind one. If the trees are well spaced out then there may be a way back to the fairway or onto the green, but on many courses that isn't the case. The golfer is therefore faced with the option of chipping out sideways, through a safe gap and sacrificing a stroke, or trying a more difficult shot through a gap a few feet wide, that will allow them to make forward progress.

Just imagine that. Having just missed a fairway that is fifty yards wide, the golfer is now going to try to thread his way through a gap five feet wide. What are the odds of making the shot?

I can tell you from experience: pretty much zero. But you can bet your life it is the option a lot of amateurs will go for. OK, sometimes it works, but many more times it doesn't. This is probably one of the biggest errors in course management that amateurs make.

The other problem is branches. These often overhang a fairway. I had a very recent experience (at the time of writing) where my ball was, effectively in the open, but the very tip of an overhanging branch interfered with my backswing. Once again, ambition outweighed skill (and sense) and instead of playing a safe shot with a short backswing, I tried to change the shape of my swing to avoid the overhanging branch. My ball was never seen again.

Even when not on the backswing, overhanging branches tend to be in the way because the golfer needs to get the ball to rise in order to gain any distance, which then allows the branches to gobble up the ball as it passes through the tree. Most times the ball will just drop straight down to finish underneath the branches, but sometimes the ball shoots off at odd angles, never to be seen again.

Occasionally, just occasionally, a ball will hit a branch and be thrown back onto the fairway, but that is rare. Treasure those moments and make a sacrifice to the golfing Gods in thanks for your good fortune.

But the leaves don't have to be on the tree to cause a problem. In the autumn, when the leaves are falling from the tree like snow during a blizzard, they are a major cause of slow play. The ball rolls beneath the leaves to become hidden, or the leaves blow over the top of the ball with the same result. You can hit your ball into the middle of the fairway and still not be able to find it because of the leaves. Of course, the greenkeepers do try to remove the leaves, but they can't be everywhere at the same time and they can't remove them as quickly as nature can replace them with fresh falls.

There is one particular type of tree that has become common on the golf course which causes additional problems; the Leylandii. Anyone who has seen a hedge of these trees knows how thick they grow. A ball flying into one is likely to lodge in the foliage rather than drop to the ground, making it impossible to find. Even if they do drop, the thickness of foliage around the base still makes the ball impossible to locate. They are evil and greenkeepers that plant them are the spawn of Satan.

I think you can safely say I'm not a big fan of trees, which is why I love links courses. But as I live close to the centre of England, as far from the sea in any directions as it is possible to be, I have to play my golf on courses with trees.

But in the autumn, when the trees are turning a hundred shades of red and gold, there is no more beautiful sight in the world than a tree lined golf course.

Trees present a problem for the golfer.

Trophies

Trophies are things that other people win.

Actually that isn't true. I have won my share of trophies over the years, more so since playing with the seniors where the field is more limited, but I have won trophies for men's section competitions as well and my handicap has never been lower than 20. Anyone can win a trophy on the day they play their best golf. Sadly, those days are few and far between for most amateurs and the majority of trophies go to the best golfers in the club. Which is pretty much what you might expect.

For this reason, the "Monthly Medal" competitions are usually contested on a divisional basis. The membership is divided into divisions based on their handicaps. In our club there are three divisions for the men's section and two for the seniors. With my handicap it means I am division 3 for a men's section medal competitions and division 2 for a seniors' medal. And the prize for winning or being runner-up really is a medal; it's usually about two inches across and there is even a little hole by which it can be attached to a ribbon (but never is).

Other than medals, there are two sorts of trophy. The first is the big shiny silver, crystal or cut-glass ones that are kept locked up in back-lit, glass fronted cabinets in the clubhouse. They are removed for the sole purpose of handing them to the winner, before being put back under lock and key again. If the winner is lucky their name will be engraved on the trophy at the end of the year.

The other sort of trophy is the one that the winning golfer gets to keep as a memento of their win. The general rule with regard to these is that they are ugly and the golfer's spouse will ban them from any part of the home where they may be visible to visitors. The only exception to this rule is where both partners play golf and so both want their trophies displayed. Mine are on display only because my wife and I play skittles and my wife wants her skittles trophy (equally ugly) on display.

U is For

Under club or under clubbing

A minor affliction suffered by amateurs where they tend to think they can hit a ball further than they actually can. This causes them to choose a club too "small" for the shot they want to make which, in turn, leaves them short of where they wanted to be, whether it be the green or just a certain position on the fairway.

In the worst scenarios, the under-clubbing results in the ball landing in a hazard mid-way between themselves and their objective.

This phenomenon is particularly common in the late autumn and early winter, when weather conditions are changing and affect the distance the ball will travel (balls fly farther in warm thin air than in cold thick air). A golfer who can quite happily hit a ball a hundred and fifty yards with a seven iron in the summer will suddenly find the ball stopping after one hundred and thirty yards or less. If there just happens to be a bunker or water there, then it is inevitable that the ball will go into it.

You would think that the amateur would learn from that and adjust their club selections the following year, but they never do.

Up and Down

To hole the ball in two strokes from any position, i.e. from off the green. This doesn't apply to two strokes on the putting green itself.

A good "up and down" is usually what allows amateurs with high handicaps to score pars.

V is For

Vardon grip

A method of holding the club with an overlapping grip, developed by a golfer called Harry Vardon (1870 - 1937).

It is one of the three most popular styles of grip in golf, the other two being "interlocking" and "ten fingered".

W is For

Warm Up

Professional athletes, including golfers, warm up before competitions to get the blood circulating and muscles oxygenated in preparation for what is to come. It reduces the risk of muscular injuries, provides a degree of mental preparation and helps the golfer to "get their eye in".

But we amateurs wouldn't want to spoil the fun of hitting our first tee-shot out of bounds and pulling a muscle in the process, so we rarely do it.

Water

Water is the second type of hazard to be encountered on the golf course. Since 2019 it has been known as a "penalty area" rather than as a hazard, but old habits are hard to change. Golfers taking up the game in future years will probably look at us elder statesmen of the game with puzzlement when we use these archaic terms.

So, water that used to be called "lateral water" and which generally ran down the sides of holes parallel to the fairway, no longer exists. Now they are either red penalty areas or yellow penalty areas and are marked with stakes of the appropriate colours and sometimes with painted lines. If they are unmarked they are treated as red.

Knowing which is which is important, because the rules for taking relief, should you land in the penalty area, are different. Both result in a penalty being incurred, but it is where the replacement ball may be dropped that is different in the two cases.

Which brings us to "temptation".

Every golf fan in the world will remember French golfer Jean van der Velde at the 1999 Open, held at St Andrews that year. On the final hole, with an unassailable lead, he put his ball into the Barry Burn with his second shot, which was played out of thick rough. Then he put his next ball into the water. Then he put his next ball into the water (no, that isn't repeated text). Now, having used up his leader's cushion of strokes in hand, he was faced with the dilemma - what to do next. He took off his shoes and socks and climbed down the side of the burn, considering playing his ball out of the water. He thought about it for a long time, but finally saw sense, took a penalty drop and played another ball. But his visits to the water put him into a three-way play-off with Justin Leonard and Paul Lawrie, which Lawrie won. Had he taken a penalty drop in the drop zone after he first landed in the water, he would have won The Open at a canter but, instead, he fell victim to temptation.

I think most amateurs can sympathise with this dilemma. I have, on more than one occasion, been showered with water having opted to play the ball from where it was. It rarely works. Take the penalty drop, move on and hope to recover the lost strokes later in the round.

But earlier in the book I promised to tell you about a particularly notable occasion when I fell foul of the dreaded H_2O.

It was many years ago, when I was still relatively new to the game of golf. For several weeks the greenkeepers had been working on an old shallow depression which everyone called a pond but it wasn't; at least in summer it wasn't because it dried out. Now it had been converted into a proper pond, complete with fish (the fish actually came later, transported in by nature and people looking to get rid of unwanted pets).

It was the biggest golfing day of the year: Captain's Day. For weeks the new pond had been designated GUR, but at last it was introduced into play for the big day.

Up to that point I had been playing well and looked forward to being in a good position at the end of the round. Not a prize winner (it hadn't been that good), but certainly respectably placed. I took my tee shot and drove off the tee, landing perilously close to the new pond, but not actually in it. I took out my 3 wood and played my next shot. Swish, splash, damn! Drop another ball. Swish, splash, damn! Drop another ball. Swish, splash, damn! Drop another ball.

In all, seven balls met their watery end before I decided to give up and walk on down the fairway in pursuit of my partners who were, unsurprisingly, in hysterics. It was a stroke-play competition, so by not completing the hole I was defaulting to a "nil return". Not that it mattered at that point, of course. Like Jean Van der Velde, I had met my watery nemesis.

Why hadn't I taken a club that was easier to use than a 3 wood (not my favourite club at the best of times)? I have no idea. But that's what amateurs do!

There is one type of water where the golfer can take relief without incurring a penalty. That is temporary water.

Temporary water, more often called by its previous name of "casual water", is any water that isn't part of the course. This usually means puddles and saturated ground of the sort encountered in winter. However, a sudden summer squall can introduce temporary water into the game as well. Knowing the rules for playing temporary water can not only save you strokes during your round, they can also save you from getting showered in water or splattered in mud.

I can recount two incidents where partners of mine have had a problem with water, coincidentally both on the same hole.

Our 9th hole is a dog leg that goes downhill from the tee to a pond, before turning a corner to go back uphill to the green. The bigger hitters are able to clear the pond from the tee, but us mere mortals tend to lay up (see *Lay up*). The disadvantage of laying up is that it turns a par 4 hole into a par 5. But the hole has a low stroke index, so high handicap golfers can score a six and still count it as a par.

But it is also not unknown for one's second shot to go into the water. This leads the golfer into temptation.

The temptation is to climb down the rather steep bank to try to retrieve a ball that is lying enticingly close to the edge of the pond. The trouble is that the edge isn't the edge. The edge is just grass that is concealing the water beneath.

So, on the first occasion, my partner starts down the bank, only to find himself sliding uncontrollably towards the water's edge. The further he slides, the louder I laugh. He ended up knee deep in the water and I had to use my putter to extend my reach and pull him out. The irony was that he wasn't trying to retrieve his own ball, which was safely on the fairway on the far side of the water, he was trying to retrieve the balls lost by other golfers who were too sensible to attempt retrieval.

On the second occasion, a different partner (and Seniors Captain at the time) tried to retrieve his ball from the water and clambered down the bank despite the warnings of his partners, myself included, not to do so. He stepped onto what he thought was grass but was really just grass concealing a foot of water. He was now not only wet up to his knees, but he couldn't maintain his balance. He fell forward, landing with his arms well past his elbows in the water and spraying more water over himself. He too had to be helped out. Passing the clubhouse on the way to the tenth hole he decided he was too wet to continue and abandoned his round.

You have been warned!

Try to stay out of water.

Wind

The most difficult weather condition with which to have to contend. When it rains you can call off the game, often to the relief of your playing partners (though they won't admit it). But if you cancel because of the wind everyone will think you are a wimp.

The wind interferes with the flight of a golf ball quite dramatically. You wouldn't think it could affect something that is only one point six eight inches in diameter, but it does.

Hitting into the wind two things happen. First of all, the distance is reduced by the wind's resistance to the ball. Secondly, any deviation from a straight line is exaggerated as the wind pushes the ball further offline. I have seen shots turned at an angle of ninety degrees by a headwind.

A crosswind has the same effect as a head wind in terms of pushing a ball offline. The only difference is that a crosswind will push the ball even further off its intended course.

The only time that the wind is helpful is when it is directly behind, when the golfer can hope to gain increased distance, often thirty or forty yards when the wind is at its strongest.

It is yet another immutable rule of golf, but no matter which way you turn on a golf course, the wind will always be in your face or across you when you come to play your shot, even though it was behind you thirty seconds earlier.

See also F*latulence*.

Winter

Golf is a summer game which amateurs insist on playing in winter, aided and abetted by their golf club management.

This is not something that affects professionals. As soon as the Alfred Dunhill Links Championship finishes in October, the pro circus folds up its tents and heads for southern Europe. From there the players either take a well-earned break until the tour re-starts, or they go and play in even sunnier climes in the Persian Gulf, Asia, South Africa and/or Australia. As I write, in January 2020, the Abu Dhabi HSBC Championship* has just concluded and the next European Tour event is in Saudi Arabia.

But, unless you happen to have a villa in Spain or you're a millionaire (or both), this isn't an option for most amateurs.

So, we play on waterlogged courses, in fog or in thick frost, on greens that are bumpy where they aren't sodden, in bunkers that are half full of water and where a significant part of the golf course is roped off to prevent damage. I have even played golf when there was six inches of snow on the ground.

The course in question had cleared the snow off small areas of the greens so we could putt. The rest was up to us. As can be imagined, many golf balls were never seen again. Not because they were white - we weren't that stupid, we did play with brightly coloured balls - but because once the ball hit the snow it tended to bury itself and if you couldn't find the entry hole, there was no chance of finding the ball.

OK, that was a once in a lifetime experience and even my own club closes when there is snow covering the ground, but other than that they are likely to stay open.

I said in the first paragraph of this section that we are aided and abetted in this by the golf clubs and we are. They have to make money all year round if they want to stay in business, so instead of closing for the worst of the winter, which would be sensible to protect the course, they continue to operate.** Membership fees would have to be reduced if we members couldn't play in winter, so that would be a further financial blow to already beleaguered golf clubs.

Our club does try to protect the greens by putting in "winter greens" - closely mowed areas of the fairway with over-sized holes for us to play into, but that serves mainly to shorten an already short course. It doesn't protect the rest of the golf course from damage.

OK, we don't have to play in winter, but on a day like today, with the sun shining brightly, the temptation is there. The temperature may be just above freezing, but the golf clothing manufacturers do produce some excellent thermal clothing these days (see, even they are enabling our addiction). Even the R&A allows golf clubs to introduce special rules for winter golf. These allow the golfer to pick their ball up and clean it before placing it back on the ground. Cleaning the ball is an essential of winter golf and it's another reason why golfers carry a towel, because a mud caked ball is never going to fly true - or far.

So, we slosh through the water and the mud, we gain six inches in height as we walk down the fairway because the frost clings to the spikes on our shoes. Our golf balls only fly half the distance because a cold ball doesn't fly as far as a warm one and we suffer a whole host of other constraints that only inflict themselves on winter golfers.

And all the time we convince ourselves that we're either having fun, or we're doing something that is preferable to some alternative. My "go-to" alternative that I would rather not be doing is shopping with my wife, even though my wife stopped asking me to go shopping with her years ago because I moaned so much that I was spoiling her pleasure.

There are some conditions even I won't play in. I won't play in the rain, but that applies in summer as well as in winter. But that is a relatively recent development, brought on by advancing age.

So, if you see a golfer out in the winter, remember that he is more to be pitied than scorned. And it could be worse, he could be out fishing instead!

* It was won by Lee Westwood, which means he has now won tournaments in four successive decades.

** Covid-19 forced the closure of our club between mid-March and mid-May and it was incredible the beneficial effect this had on the course by the time we returned to golf.

Winter golf.

<u>Wood</u>

An obsolete term because woods are now made of metal. Anyone still playing with genuine wooden clubs would be better off gifting them to a golfing museum.

    Also the material that sends your ball flying in unexpected directions when you hit a tree. The club most likely to produce this result is a tree wood.

Boom tish!

X is For

X-Out Ball

Balls that fail the manufacturer's quality checks sometimes have their logos over-stamped with Xs and are sold off cheaply. Some have just as good performance characteristics as the balls that pass the quality test, but this isn't guaranteed.

But I have seen a ball recently that had "Cross-out" stamped on it as a logo in its own right, which presumably was a marketing ploy.

Y is For

Yardage Marker

See "Distance markers".

Yips

A golfing affliction unique to putting. The golfer tends to make an upwards jerky sort of motion with their body when striking the ball, which affects both length and accuracy. It is caused by lack of confidence in the ability to sink the putt, which becomes a self-fulfilling prophesy.

Z is For

Zip

I include this only because without it I would have had to call this book "The A to Y of (Amateur) Golf" which would have been a bit silly. Actually, including "Yardage marker" and "yips" are only to avoid having to call the book the A to X of (Amateur) Golf. And then there's X … (**Editor's note**: OK, we get the idea. Just get on with it).

It had been my intention to insert the name of a golf club or course that started with the letter Z, but I couldn't find one. If you do know of one, please let me know and I'll include it in the next edition of this book.

So, zip could be the method of keeping a jacket or the pocket of a golf bag closed.

In American golfing parlance it actually means the spin imparted onto a ball when it is struck. Personally, I just call this "spin", but golfers love to give different names to things, so I'm happy to include zip as the concluding entry in this book.

Final Words

This book is incomplete and I know it is incomplete. No matter often I update it, it will always remain incomplete, because as fast as I can capture one bit of jargon or terminology, someone comes along and invents another. So, my apologies if you have come here looking for an explanation for a word, humorous or otherwise and been unable to find it, but I'll do my best to capture it for future editions if you let me know what it is (*see Final Words for contact information*).

From this book you might get the idea that I don't actually like golf much. Nothing could be further from the truth. But what is true is that I have a bit of a love-hate relationship with the game, which I think is true for many amateurs.

On a fine day in summer, when I'm playing my best game, there is no finer way, in my humble opinion, of spending several hours in good company.

But on a damp morning in January, with water seeping over the top of my shoes and unable to hit a decent shot to save my life, you can imagine that I'm not so much in love with the game.

While we may be able to forecast what the weather conditions might be, the one thing we can never forecast is how well we will play on any given day. I have crawled out of my bed in the winter darkness, not wishing to turn on the light out of consideration for my sleeping wife and driven to the golf club feeling that I really should have turned over and gone back to sleep while I still had the chance. But on arrival I've played some of the best golf I've ever played.

And on a fine sunny day, when all the course conditions have been right and I've felt that today was going to be a good day of golf - I've sliced my tee shot from the 1st onto the 18th fairway and ended up scoring a 9 on the opening hole.

You can never tell what is going to happen, which is the great fascination of golf.

The game itself is the challenge, not the people you play against. The people who are present make the game more sociable, that's all.

Yes, I enter competitions because I want to win them, but at the end of the round it is my own score that is of most interest to me, not what the other competitors have scored. Did I play my best or did I let myself down? Every game of golf consists of two competitors, even when playing by yourself. It is you versus the golf course. Did the course beat me, or did I beat the course?

And thirty minutes later, when I've got myself on the outside a pint of beer and a plate of chips, it won't matter either way. Which is when I remind myself that there's always next time.

Yes, there is always the next round, which may be the day I hit peak performance and play the best round I will ever play. And when that happens, I'll finally hang up my clubs, because there will no longer be any reason to play again.

No, I'm lying, because I will return to see if I can beat that perfect round, even though it may be a fruitless endeavour.

And when my time is over and I go to that great golf course in the sky, St Peter will have a tee-off time booked for me to play and my partners will be Arnold Palmer, Bobby Jones and Young Tom Morris and we will play on a course that resembles Augusta or St Andrews.

But please, don't make it for this weekend as I've got a tee-off time booked at my own club. *

I'll leave the final, final words with that great golfer, Obi Wan Kenobi. "May the course be with you."

* **Publisher's note**: Just for the sake of clarity, this was delayed until after the Covid-19 social distancing restrictions were relaxed to allow the playing of golf once again. We have to hope that St Peter is prepared to wait.

I've got a tee tee-time booked.

Acknowledgements

No book is ever the work of a single person, even though only the author's name appears on the cover. Other people make their contributions in myriad ways. So it is time to say thank you.

First of all, my thanks go to Ivan Zamyslov, a young Latvian who I have never met but who did all the illustrations for me.

Secondly, my thanks go to fellow golfer Andy Burgess for beta reading this book and providing feedback which has helped to improve it - as well as pointing out that Bobby Jones was an amateur golfer, not a professional as I had thought.

Thirdly, thank you to my publisher, Robert Agar-Hutton, who actually suggested that I write a book about golf. I'm not sure if this is what he had in mind, but it is what he got and it is now his job to try and make some money out of it for both of us.

My thanks must also go to Peter Mark Roget (1779-1869) for including the word "immutable" in his esteemed thesaurus.

Finally, my thanks go to those hundreds of golfers who have accompanied me around the golf course over the last 40 years and whose stories and experiences have, not that they may ever know it, helped to inform this book. Without them the game of golf would be a very lonely and tedious pastime. May their drives be straight and true and may their putts always drop for them.

Sources

The following sources were used in compiling this book, They are listed in no particular order, but may have been used on more than one occasion within the book:

https://www.randa.org/en/rog/2019/pages/the-rules-of-golf

https://www.scottishgolfhistory.org/origin-of-golf-terms/

https://golftips.golfweek.com/meaning-albatross-golf-20123.html

https://www.golfmagic.com/golf-news/golfer-follows-albatross-21-par-4

https://en.wikipedia.org/wiki/Main_Page
(Unsurprisingly, Wikipedia has provided the source for quite a lot of the research in relation to this book, too many to link to individual entries.)

https://www.golfdigest.com/story/comparing-your-handicap-index

https://www.englandgolf.org/

https://www.usga.org/

https://www.thestandrewsgolfclub.co.uk/

https://www.thesportshistorian.com/a-short-history-of-the-british-open/

https://www.historic-uk.com/HistoryUK/HistoryofScotland/The-History-of-Golf/

https://www.liveabout.com/origin-of-the-word-mulligan-1561085

https://www.pga.info/

https://www.core77.com/posts/25240/A-Brief-History-of-Golf-Ball-Design-and-Why-You-Shouldnt-Hit-People-with-Baseball-Bats

https://www.scottishgolfhistory.org/oldest-golf-clubs-societies/

https://www.randa.org/en/rulesequipment/pace-of-play/overview

And Now

Both the author Robert Cubitt and Selfishgenie Publishing hope that you have enjoyed reading this story.

Please tell people about this eBook, write a review on Amazon or mention it on your favourite social networking site. Word of mouth is an author's best friend and is much appreciated. Thank you.
Find Robert Cubitt on Facebook at https://www.facebook.com/robertocubitt and 'like' his page; follow him on Twitter **@Robert_Cubitt**

For further titles that may be of interest to you please visit our website at **selfishgenie.com** where you can optionally join our information list.

Printed in Great Britain
by Amazon